THE RED AND THE BLACK

Studies in Greek pottery

Brian A. Sparkes

ROUTLEDGE

London and New York

First published 1996
by Routledge
11 New Fetter Lane, London EC4P 4EE

Simultaneously published in the USA and Canada
by Routledge
29 West 35th Street, New York, NY 10001

Routledge is an International Thomson Publishing company

© 1996 Brian A. Sparkes

Typeset in Garamond by
Florencetype Ltd, Stoodleigh, Devon

Printed and bound in Great Britain by
Redwood Books, Trowbridge, Wiltshire

British Library Cataloguing in Publication Data
A catalogue record for this book is available from the British Library

Library of Congress Cataloguing in Publication Data
Sparkes, Brian A.
The red and the black: studies in Greek pottery/Brian A. Sparkes
p.   cm.
ISBN 0–415–12660–6 (HB). – ISBN 0–415–12661–4 (PB)
1. Vases, Red-figured – Greece. 2. Vases, Black-figured – Greece.
3. Vases, Greek. I. Title.
NK4649.S68   1996
738.3'82'0938–dc20   95–40622
CIP

ISBN 0–415–12660–6 (hbk)
ISBN 0–415–12661–4 (pbk)

THE RED AND THE BLACK

OWL

Greek painted pottery fetches high prices on the art market of today. The vases are very collectable, with their attractive shapes, decoration and figured scenes, with some carrying the signatures of individual craftsmen. *The Red and the Black* looks at the stages which have led to this enthusiastic urge to buy, and sets it against the history and significance of pottery production in ancient Greece.

In providing an accessible account of the production of pottery in ancient Greece,

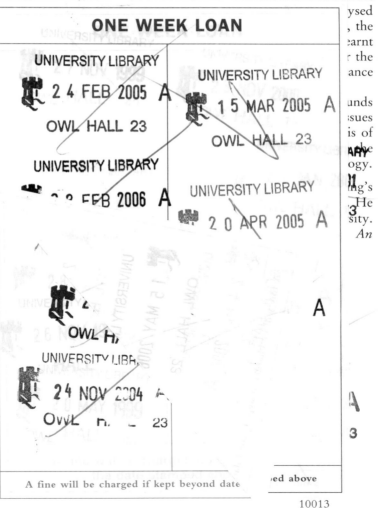

...ysed with m... location... about t... history... to the... Bria... of tradi... involve... as much student...

Brian A... College... is curre... His m... *Introdu...*

...the... ...unds ...sues is of ...ARY ...ogy. ...ng's ...He ...sity. *An*

To the memory of
Lucy Talcott
(1899–1970)
and
Alison Frantz
(1903–1995)

CONTENTS

———— ·◆· ————

ILLUSTRATIONS

———— •◆• ————

The following list gives information, where possible, on the origin, shape, subject matter, date, findspot, size, and present location, together with a reference to a recent publication, either with a published photograph and discussion and/or a reference to further illustrations and discussion. The sources of the photographs are also listed. I am grateful to all museums and individuals who have supplied the material and granted permission for publication.

PREFACE

———— •◆• ————

The chapters in this book are based on the lectures that I gave at the University of Aberdeen during the early months of 1992, when holding the Geddes-Harrower Chair of Classical Art and Archaeology. I am very grateful to the University for inviting me to speak there and for the hospitality extended to me when I was in residence. I am particularly grateful to Patrick Edwards, John Fraser and Liz Weir, of King's College.

Some of the lectures have been delivered on other occasions, and I have benefited from comments and new information offered to me from time to time. I am also grateful for the critical remarks made by the two anonymous readers to whom the text of the lectures was sent by the publishers.

Transfer from the lecture format to the page is never easy, and there have naturally been changes: fewer illustrations, expansion of certain aspects for which there was no time in the lecture hours at my disposal, a rather less jaunty style. However, I hope I have retained some of the flavour of the occasions. The chapters have emerged with an art-historical bias, but that at least suits one aspect of the professorial title under which the lectures were delivered. For the emphasis on Athens there is no similar excuse. This is not a book for professional students of Greek pottery, but for those who are less acquainted with the subject, its pleasures and its personalities (ancient and modern).

The bibliography, now it is finished, looks more daunting than I had wanted it to be; it is intended to direct readers to more extended treatments of some of the themes. I have also listed an annotated selection of useful books and articles at the end of each chapter.

I have given a detailed list of illustrations on pp. viii–xxi, and I am grateful to all the museum curators and private owners who have given me permission to publish the photographs. I hope that I have been punctilious in chasing up permissions; for those I have missed, my apologies. I am also grateful to the Carcanet Press for permission to quote from Robert Graves's poem 'Ogres and Pygmies'.

I have received much help from Vicky Peters and Joanne Snooks of the Routledge staff and from Hannah Hyam whose copy-editing eye saved me from many sins of commission and omission.

I owe a deep debt of gratitude to the University of Southampton for a grant to cover the costs of the illustrations. The drawings and profiles were executed by Alan Burn and his team in the Cartographic Unit of the University; my thanks to them.

The dedication expresses my appreciation to two of the central figures in the American excavations of the Athenian Agora, Lucy Talcott and Alison Frantz: for many years they both helped to make young scholars, of whatever nationality, feel that they were an important part of the academic fellowship there. They are sadly missed.

BAS
June 1995

ABBREVIATIONS

——— •◆• ———

PUBLICATIONS

AA	*Archäologischer Anzeiger*
ABSA	*Annual of the British School at Athens*
AJA	*American Journal of Archaeology*
AK	*Antike Kunst*
AM	*Athenische Mitteilungen*
AMI	*Archaeologische Mitteilungen aus Iran*
Arch. News	*Archaeological News*
BABesch	*Bulletin Antieke Beschaving*
BCH	*Bulletin de Correspondance Hellénique*
BICS	*Bulletin of the Institute of Classical Studies*
CAJ	*Cambridge Archaeological Journal*
CIL	*Corpus Inscriptionum Latinarum*
CR	*Classical Review*
CVA	*Corpus Vasorum Antiquorum*
GettyMusJ	*The J. Paul Getty Museum Journal*
JDAI	*Jahrbuch des Deutschen Archäologischen Instituts*
JHS	*Journal of Hellenic Studies*
JRA	*Journal of Roman Archaeology*
JWCI	*Journal of the Warburg and Courtauld Institutes*
MJbK	*Münchener Jahrbuch der bildenden Kunst*
MMA Bulletin	*Bulletin of the Metropolitan Museum of Art*
OJA	*Oxford Journal of Archaeology*
PBA	*Proceedings of the British Academy*
PBSR	*Papers of the British School at Rome*
PCPS	*Proceedings of the Cambridge Philological Society*
RA	*Revue Archéologique*
RM	*Römische Mitteilungen*

MUSEUMS

Aegina	Aegina, Museum
Getty	Malibu, The J. Paul Getty Museum

London BM	London, British Museum
Munich	Munich, Staatliche Antikensammlungen
Oxford	Oxford, The Ashmolean Museum
Vatican	Rome, Vatican Museum

TIMELINE

———— •◆• ————

There is no direct line that links Greek pottery with absolute chronology; all the connections are by indirect association (see Sparkes 1991a: chapter II). Early dates are approximate.

1250–1150	Destruction of Mycenaean and other east Mediterranean civilisations.
1100–1050	Sub-Mycenaean pottery.
1050–950	Migration of Greek mainlanders to Aegean islands and west coast of Asia Minor. Widespread use of iron begins.
1050–900	Protogeometric pottery.
900–700	Geometric pottery.
776	Traditional date for first Olympic Games.
750–700	*Iliad* and *Odyssey* of Homer; Hesiod.
	Adoption of alphabet from Phoenicia.
	Start of settlement ('colonisation') abroad.
725–600	Orientalising pottery.
725–625	Protocorinthian pottery.
610	Start of Athenian black-figure pottery.
566	Reorganisation of Panathenaic festival at Athens.
546	Persian conquest of Lydia and East Greece. Greek refugees go west.
530	Start of Athenian red-figure pottery.
499–494	Ionian revolt from Persia.
490	First Persian expedition against Greece (Darius).
	Battle at Marathon.
480–479	Second Persian expedition (Xerxes).
	Battles at Artemisium, Thermopylae, Salamis, Plataea and Mykale.
	Sack of Athens.
478	Delian League founded by Athens.
467	Battle of Eurymedon.
449	Peace of Callias.
447	The building of the Parthenon at Athens started.
431–404	Peloponnesian War between Athens and Sparta and their allies.
421	Peace of Nicias.

415   Athenian expedition against Sicily.
      Mutilation of Herms and Profanation of Mysteries.
404   Athens capitulates.
399   Trial and execution of Socrates.
359   Philip II becomes King of Macedon.
348   Sack of Olynthus by Philip.
338   Philip ends Greek independence.
336   Assassination of Philip and accession of Alexander.
334–323   Alexander's years of conquest.
331   Foundation of Alexandria.
323   Death of Alexander.
      Creation of Hellenistic kingdoms begins.
263   Eumenes founds the kingdom of Pergamum.
196   Rome declares the freedom of Greece.
167   Battle of Pydna ends the kingdom of Macedon.
146   Corinth sacked, and Carthage destroyed.
      Macedonia becomes a Roman province.
133   Pergamene kingdom becomes Roman province of Asia.
66–63   Creation of provinces of Bithynia, Cilicia, Syria and Crete.
30   Annexation of Egypt by Rome.

CHAPTER I

'THAT GREAT CURSE OF ARCHAEOLOGY'

———— •◆• ————

INTRODUCTION

The title of this first chapter is taken from an article by Moses Finley entitled 'Technical innovation and economic progress in the ancient world' (1965: 41; 1983: 190). The whole sentence reads 'We are too often victims of that great curse of archaeology, the indestructibility of pots.' More recently, pottery has been dubbed an 'archaeological "black hole"' (Orton, Tyers and Vince 1993: 3). The pots may shatter, but the pieces remain, accidental survivors of the whole. This is certainly true in the case of Greek pottery – excavation tables and museum shelves attest to its truth.

Students of the ancient world have been quick to appreciate the advantages that the survival of Greek pottery has brought. Its very presence marks sites, helps to distinguish the varied uses in different areas, indicates the spread of Greek contact within and beyond the Mediterranean, assists in dating rarer surviving materials. In itself, it provides information on techniques of manufacture, and the different shapes that were fashioned enable functions to be revealed. Where the pots carry decoration, particularly painted figures and figured scenes, the images can be studied for what they disclose of aspects of everyday life, and of the varieties of myth that can be contrasted with those that survive in texts. The images may also suggest reflections deeper than the surface appearance. In the absence of the more important panel painting, the very painting on the pottery has been seen as an aid to appreciating its development.

So why a 'great curse', why a 'black hole'? There are various aspects to the curse. First, pots by their very survival are given a higher profile and greater importance than they had in antiquity, where they received barely a mention. Attention has recently been drawn to the fetishism that objects, in this case handsome Greek vases, create (Spivey 1991: 134), and hence they have been elevated beyond their status. Second, their present numbers have led to a need to classify them, to systematise them, to tame them, as it were. The danger is there that once ticketed, grouped, dated, pigeonholed, computerised into a data bank, the job may be counted done, when the task has only just started. Third, this has often led to pottery being considered a subject on its own, unrelated to the contexts of production or function, divorced from the political, social and economic background within which the vases were produced. Fourth, pottery is treated as a touchstone by which to measure other objects. Greek painted pottery has had an added problem in that its very attractiveness – the shapes, the original decoration, the subject matter of its figured scenes – has unbalanced its study; and even within that framework, some pottery, either by its very attractiveness, its susceptibility to the connoisseurship approach or the usefulness of its images vis-à-vis the textual evidence from classical antiquity, has been more intensively studied than others. A wide gap has appeared. Emphasis has been placed on the art-historical aspect; the vases have attracted the art-market approach (as well as the art market), even though Greek vases do not seem to have been considered, at the time of their making, as works of art, objects to be admired in their own right. The subjects painted do indeed give us a helpful glimpse into the development of figure drawing and the popular images of Greek experience, whether of myth, everyday life or imagination. This emphasis has given them a museum orientation, torn from their contexts and set amongst their kind; the historical development of the study has helped to fix the lines of approach (see Chapter II). The quality of the pottery has also tended to direct the attention of scholars to the production end of the ceramic spectrum and has encouraged them to pay less attention to the role of the consumer.

All this has given the vases an appeal to students of classical literature, mythology and history who are looking for visual substantiation of their own studies. Such an appeal is not likely to wane, but parameters on the conclusions to be derived from the comparison are now more strictly drawn. For archaeologists not reared on a detailed study of the classical world in the traditional way of language and literature, the questions to be asked and answered are different. Classicists look more to the immediate foreground, with its accent on individuals and historical development; archaeologists have their eyes fixed more firmly on the slow-moving background. But the terms 'classicists' and 'archaeologists' are not sufficiently precise; within those categories there lurk the students of Greek religion, the social and economic historians, the archaeometrists, the statisticians. Depending on the approach, Greek pottery will be studied for itself (technique, use, price, contents, etc.) or for external reasons (contexts, art, myth, life). Greek pottery belongs to no single camp: it serves many purposes in the attempts that are made to construct a clearer picture of the Greek world.

ORGANISATION

This book is organised in six chapters, each with a different approach. This initial chapter sets the scene and presents a summary history of Greek pottery in the traditional manner, with the main emphasis on the painted and figured wares in different parts of Greece. The four chapters which follow take specific themes. The second chapter looks at the history of the interest in Greek vases, as the present balance of its study derives to a large extent from the way in which Greek pottery has been studied and collected since the Renaissance. The third chapter presents the vases from the points of view of the consumer: who handled them, who ordered them, what their purpose was. The fourth and fifth chapters look at the vases from the points of view of the makers and the subjects. The last chapter considers a variety of modern concerns that have been the subject of recent polemic and interest.

DECORATED POTTERY

Early Iron Age (c. 1100–c. 700 BC)

In a traditional treatment of Greek pottery it is usual to consider the pots from the viewpoint of source of production and to concentrate on the decorated pieces, to gain a bird's eye view of the various centres that were located in different areas of the Greek world. The Early Iron Age encompasses the products of the early centuries of the first millennium BC, roughly 1100–700 BC. This was the time when the Greeks were climbing back from the collapse of the Late Bronze Age which had seen the Mycenaean palace system, which had developed during the second millennium, reach its apogee and then be destroyed. Pottery provides the fullest information on which we can base an understanding of developments at that time. Although most of the outstanding elements of the earlier culture (palaces, writing, foreign contacts, etc.) had disappeared, more basic needs continued, and among those basic needs was pottery. Potters were adapting the old shapes and introducing new patterns of decoration. There is a poorly evidenced period of transition, termed the Sub-Mycenaean, which is marked by slack shapes and ineffectual decoration, and this is followed by the Protogeometric period (c. 1050–900 BC) (Desborough 1952; 1972; Snodgrass 1971; Murray 1975). The century and a half shows how slow-moving the development in both shapes and decoration was. The painter's approach to decoration was fairly uniform, but with local variation; patterns were sparse and austere (mainly circles and semi-circles), and much of the surface was covered in black.

The Geometric patterning multiplied in the succeeding Geometric period (c. 900–700 BC): lines, dots, zigzags, hatching, deriving in part from containers in other materials such as woven baskets, woodwork and textiles, and this patterning has given its name to the period in which it was produced (Coldstream 1968; Schweitzer 1971; Hurwit 1993). What is for archaeologists the Early Iron Age is for historians of pottery the Geometric period. The pottery is more numerous and more widely distributed than earlier. Initial austerity gave way to more complex designs, but always in a controlled, linear and rectilinear manner, with the use of compass and multiple brush. The fired colour of the paint is dark brown on the lighter surface of the pot and emphasises and enhances the shape, whether open, for example cups, or closed, for example amphorae.

Most of the pottery recovered comes from grave contexts, some buried as ash urns for the cremated remains of the dead, others laid in the grave as offerings, either for the inhumed or for the cremated. Towards the end of the period (eighth century) some aristocratic graves in one of the cemeteries in Athens were marked above ground by monumental vases (amphorae and kraters), sometimes as much as 1.25 m high, over 4 ft (Figure I: 1a). Some carried on their surface figured narrative scenes of death and burial: *prothesis* or the laying out of the dead, and *ekphora* or the procession to the grave (Coldstream 1991). Earlier, single figures of animals and humans had been inserted into the geometric patterning, both at Athens and elsewhere, and the question of possible continuity from the Bronze Age has been raised (Benson 1970; Hampe and Simon 1981; Vermeule 1991; for continuity of craftsmanship, see Papadopoulos 1994). However, it is with such narrative scenes (including fighting, hunting, ships and mourning) at this time (*c.* 750–700 BC) that the beginnings of figured drawing and painting in narrative form are first encountered (Snodgrass 1979; 1980; 1987: chapter 5). The potter was an important craftsman and was being given commissions to shape such funerary memorials. There was no large-scale sculpture being carved at this time, nor for over a century to come; the impressive grave markers were the most monumental forms being made. Controlled and precise, the painted figures take the form of their shape and the direction of their gestures from the surrounding pattern. The solid, angular silhouettes express their grief and honour their dead with hands to head before the funeral couch (Figure I: 1b). The black paint is interlaced with the orange of the clay background in a sober and harmonious scheme, and this contrast of black skin and orange body is maintained in the following centuries – the variation is derived from the way in which the figures and the decoration are presented (Mertens 1988).

The leader at this time seems to have been Athens; other areas of Greece also produced similar shapes and decoration, more or less influenced by Athenian work but with their own local accents and choice of subject (Coldstream 1968 and 1991), for example Euboea (Boardman 1952, and cf. Kearsley 1989); Argos (Courbin 1966); Corinth; Boeotia (Ruckert 1976); Crete; the Cyclades.

Orientalising (*c.* 725–*c.* 600 BC)

By the following century (700–600 BC) changes are obvious. Contact with the craftsmen of the Near East and with their arts (e.g. ivory, metal and textiles), a contact that had been growing with the expansion of the Greek

Figure I: 1a Athenian Geometric krater, *c.* 740 BC. Ht 72.3 cm.

Figure I: 1b Detail of Figure I: 1a.

world in the previous century, had begun to have its effect on painted pottery, both in technique, arrangement and subject (for the general influence from the East, see Burkert 1992; S.P. Morris 1992). The linear straitjacket of the Geometric style had already been shaken loose by the figured scenes of narrative and was gradually becoming looser still – full-bodied and curvaceous animals and plants (real and imaginary) take up more room than the background pattern; their silhouette shapes begin to be enlivened by incised lines (derived from the metal and ivory prototypes) and by touches of colour – mainly white and purple. This is what is now referred to as the black-figure technique. There is also some outlining of figures, which is new, but it proved less popular, perhaps because of the curve of the surface. But whether in silhouette or outline, the figures are a threat to the pattern. Shapes also had changed. The foreign influence, which seems to have reached the mainland first with lines of communication striking westwards from the island of Rhodes, was stronger and the development quicker in some centres than in others.

Corinth, a rising state with wide contacts both east and west, seems to have felt the effect first and most strongly (Payne 1931; 1933; Amyx 1988;

Figure I: 2 Protocorinthian aryballos, from Thebes, *c.* 640 BC.
Ht 6.8 cm.

Rasmussen 1991) and to have influenced other centres. Seventh-century Corinthian potters and painters are best at miniature work, especially scenes on small aryballoi (Figure I: 2) and alabastra. There are also vases that are painted in a wider range of colours (polychromy: brown for men; white for women; red), and influence from monumental painting that was starting to be produced at this time has been suggested (Broneer 1971; for a negative view, see Pemberton 1989b). Miniature work demands the discipline of precision and receives it in the earlier part of the century, but as the century proceeds, the work loses quality. Few areas were totally immune from orientalising fashions, whether one looks at the products of other mainland centres or of the islands and the Greek settlements that had developed on the coast of Asia Minor.

The normal run of decoration consisted of floral patterns, either singly or in chains, and animal friezes. But on the more elaborate pieces subjects were now more varied, and an important element that was gaining ground

Figure I: 3 Protoattic amphora, from Eleusis, *c.* 650 BC. Ht of picture 42 cm.

was that of myth (Fittschen 1969; Carter 1972) – the stories of the gods, the tales of heroes and the figures of fantasy. For instance, on more than one vase of this period Odysseus and his companions are shown blinding the giant Cyclops (e.g. Figure I: 3) – a story that was immediately recognisable from the elements given. The question arises whether Homer's *Odyssey* was now in circulation and had affected the choice of subject or whether the appearance of story and image was coincidental – what had been passed down orally was now being shown visually because figured images had begun to be created. Scenes of human life beyond the range of a funerary setting were also now beginning to show more variety.

Not all centres produced wares with human figures; many focused their work on animals, others put more stress on floral decoration, and some still retained elements of the now old-fashioned Geometric patterning. This is most noticeable in the islands, such as Chios where the surface is covered with a creamy slip (Lemos 1991), Rhodes and its neighbourhood where again a creamy slip is added and wild goats are popular figures (Figure I: 4). Other centres produce mixed styles, such as Paros (Weill and Salviat 1960) and Euboea (Boardman 1952). There are also the settlements

Figure I: 4 Rhodian Wild Goat jug, *c.* 650–640 BC. Ht 39.5 cm.

that had grown up with the emigration of Greeks to South Italy and Sicily, and these too produced their own variety of painted pottery (e.g. at Syracuse and Megara Hyblaea). The finds from these 'colonial' sites are very varied and show the mixture of imports that had a diverse effect on the local products.

Athens and the areas around (in this period her production is called Protoattic) seem to have lost impetus, and contrast sharply with Corinth in the way in which Corinth was exporting her small perfume-vases (aryballoi and alabastra) to the west and elsewhere in great quantities, whilst Athens, although potting and painting on a grander scale, was exporting very little; she was catering more for her own needs (Osborne 1989; Whitley 1994). Her work is tied more firmly to the preceding Geometric period,

9

with special-purpose grave goods, a mixture of old and new iconography, an uneasy blend of geometric and orientalising motifs, patchy use of incision, a fondness for outline, and at times a mix of techniques that produced what is called the Black and White style (e.g. Figure I: 3; S.P. Morris 1984).

Archaic (*c.* 600–*c.* 480 BC): black-figure

During the four generations that comprise the Archaic period, there is great variety in the production of pottery decorated in the black-figure technique. Local centres each had their own individual shapes and decoration, and most pots can now usually be traced back to their place of manufacture. But as the century progresses, the local centres become fewer, and even Corinthian production ceases to have any real importance after 550 BC. It is Athens that now moves forward, and with the invention and development of the red-figure technique in Athens *c.* 530 BC local production of decorated pottery at other centres is virtually at an end, maintained in a few places for special purposes.

As we saw, the potters and painters at Athens were dazzled for a few generations by the ferment of new ideas created by the influence from the East, but by the end of the seventh century they had absorbed the shock, steadied themselves and were at the start of three centuries (600–300 BC) in which they increasingly showed their skill and vitality in potting and painting (for black-figure, see Beazley 1951/1986; Boardman 1974). By whatever means and for whatever reasons, Athens dominated the scene from then on, and the other local producers of fine painted wares were minor concerns. Corinthian pottery, which had been influential in forming the Athenian style but by the sixth century had started to imitate Athenian (Amyx 1988: 539–40), is still produced in good numbers, if not good quality, in the first half of the sixth century but becomes less and less important outside its own boundaries, although the outline decoration continues later (Pemberton 1989a: 192–234). It is in the sixth century that Athenian pottery starts to be spread all over the Mediterranean and beyond.

Athenian pottery has enjoyed a privileged position in the study of Greek pottery over the last century. The quality of its well-disciplined and articulated shapes, the variety and detail of its images, the quantity of the material, and its susceptibility to art-historical handling in a stylistic sequence, have appealed to students of different disciplines. In the painted scenes human figures, and human, heroic and divine activity are paramount; all the rest is becoming subordinate to this theme. The design has been simplified and clarified, the background ornament has shrunk. The incised lines through the shiny black gloss that dig down into the orange clay below give the interior markings of the figures their liveliness and power.

In shapes, pattern and iconography Corinth exerted an influence on Athenian potters and painters of black-figure ware, and in the early years of the sixth century Athens produced close imitations of Corinthian wares. The scale, as with Corinthian figures, is small, either in rows on the large pots or as the decoration on cups (Komast, Siana, Lip, Band), with figures spread on a narrow frieze or isolated at the centre of the rim (e.g. Figure V: 1).

Animal friezes and florals, though still popular, become less important. It is human figures that attract the painters. Mythical tales and epic stories can now be more readily recognised by their specific character, their circumstantial detail, the attributes that gradually became particular to different divinities and heroes (Poseidon and his trident, Zeus and his thunderbolt, Herakles and his lionskin), and by the naming of the figures (left to right, right to left seems to make no difference at this stage). The alphabet had been the greatest gift that the Near East had bestowed on Greece, and already by the seventh century potters and painters had started to name the protagonists in their scenes. Occasionally craftsmen's names are to be found – as either potters or painters or both. An Athenian bowl (dinos/lebes) on a stand dating c. 580 BC (Figure I: 5), which shows the

Figure I: 5 Athenian black-figure dinos/lebes, c. 580 BC. Ht of figures 8 cm.

procession at the wedding of Peleus and Thetis, the parents of the hero Achilles, in figures 8 cm (3 in.) high, carries the name of the painter (in black, vertically by the column of the house): 'Sophilos', the first painter's name we have from Athens (Williams 1983a). The precise purpose of such inscriptions, whether of potter or painter, is still unclear – pride, personal preference, fashion, commercial advertisement – but they serve to under-line the individuality of manual work and remind us that each painted pot is a unique document (see Chapter IV).

Sophilos worked with small-scale figures, as did his predecessor the Gorgon Painter and his contemporary Kleitias. The famous François Vase, the earliest known volute-krater or mixing bowl (Boardman 1974: figure 46; Stewart 1983), is covered with row upon row of mythological scenes such as the killing of the Calydonian boar, the chariot race at the funeral games for the dead Patroklos, the slaughter of Troilos outside Troy, the wedding of Peleus and Thetis (again), the return of Dionysos to Olympus, etc.; only one frieze carries a parade of animals. It also carried the names of the potter (Ergotimos) and of the painter (Kleitias). A few Athenian vases of this time have been found in remoter parts of the Mediterranean; the François Vase was found in an Etruscan tomb at Chiusi (Clusium) and is a harbinger of the traffic in Athenian pottery to the Etruscans that increases as the century progresses; another of Kleitias' volute-kraters was taken to Egypt (von Bothmer 1981c). Some potters and painters of the mid-sixth century and later seem to have shaped and decorated their vases specifically for export to Etruria (Carpenter 1983 and 1984a; Rasmussen 1985; and see Chapter VI).

A generation later we have the vignettes on the lips of drinking cups – the 'Little Master' cups (c. 550–530 BC) – with mythological scenes such as the birth of Athena from the head of Zeus (Figure V: 1) or scenes of imagination such as satyrs and nymphs. Or it may be a pleasing tondo set in the centre of a cup; again these could be mythological or derived from everyday life such as a hunter returning with his catch (Boardman 1974: figure 110). The white and purple enliven the compositions, and letters – sometimes the names of craftsmen, sometimes exhortations to drink one's fill, and sometimes a nonsense sequence – are woven into the overall design (cf. Lissarrague 1992). The fact that such small scenes can be magnified many times their real size and not lose their precision says a great deal about the meticulousness of the original painting and drawing, though not all painters were equally careful.

Around the middle of the sixth century, there is a return to larger figures and to grander themes. The death of the Amazon queen Penthesileia at the hands of Achilles shows the painter Exekias at his majestic best (Figure I: 6). On this vase he is named as potter (elsewhere as painter, and some-times as both potter and painter), and the form of the amphora, which stands over 40 cm (16 in.) high and is a new version of the shape, perhaps created by Exekias himself, has a stateliness of its own – it has recently

Figure I: 6 Athenian black-figure neck-amphora, from Vulci,
c. 540–530 BC. Ht 41.6 cm.

Figure I: 7 Athenian black-figure cup (Type A), *c.* 540 BC.
Diam. 25.7 cm.

been commented that 'The body is so finely potted and the contours so tight that it almost seems as if touching the vase would either cause it to burst like a bubble or gently lift off like a balloon' (Williams 1985: 34). Earlier and later contemporaries of Exekias, such as Lydos, Nearchos, Amasis (some were potters, some painters and some both), help to extend the limits of the technique, and there are potters and painters, whose names are not known and for whom conventional sobriquets have been invented, that are their equal in quality. From inscriptions on the pots we learn that Tleson was a potter and the son of Nearchos who was himself both a potter and painter, and that Kleophrades the potter was the son of Amasis who had himself been a potter. It is still unclear whether Amasis, whom we know to have been a potter, was also a painter (von Bothmer 1985a; Mertens 1987; Isler 1994); some have seen a similarity between the individuality of the shapes and the combination of stiff formality and merriment that characterises the painter who decorated almost all Amasis' pots (Figure I: 7). That the potters and painters were known to one another can be deduced from the general similarities in style and subject matter and also from instances where they parody one another's work and mock one another (Boardman 1987a: 148–9; for names, see now Williams 1995).

Other centres produced black-figure painted pottery and variations of it during this same period. One might instance Laconian (Stibbe 1972; Pipili 1987; Margreiter 1988), a rather flat-footed style that found favour in Libya (Figure I: 8; Stibbe 1991); Boeotian (Kilinski 1990), much influenced both by Corinth and by Athens; East Greek (Langlotz 1975: 178–99; Cook 1992),

Figure I: 8 Laconian black-figure cup, *c.* 570–560 BC. Diam. 14 cm.

best known for the so called Fikellura vases found on the island of Rhodes; Caeretan (Hemelrijk 1984), a colourful and lively workshop with its centre of production in Etruria itself but with a style that indicates that the crafts-men had emigrated from Eastern Greece (Figure V: 5), most likely in response to the Persian encroachment in the middle of the century (for vase-painting in archaic Etruria under Greek influence, see Boardman 1994a: 228–41); Chiot (Lemos 1991), with a lively export to Naukratis in Egypt (Figure I: 9); Clazomenian (Cook 1981), a centre of production we know best today for the elaborately terracotta painted sarcophagi; Chalcidian (Rumpf 1927), named from the letter forms of the inscriptions that resemble those of Euboean Chalcis and in shape and decoration very like Athenian but found in the west and hence most likely produced in a Chalcidian colony in South Italy or Sicily. All can now be distinguished by such details as shape, glaze, slip, choice of subject matter, distribution, but they do not all lend themselves to the minute classification that has been accorded to the Athenian products.

Figure I: 9 Chiot bowl, from Naukratis, *c.* 600 BC. Diam. 38 cm.

Archaic (*c.* 530–*c.* 480 BC): red-figure

Black men, white women, no spatial depth, one ground line, all foreground – a bold and fitting treatment for the curving surface of a pot. But change again was on the way. As Hamlet urged his mother Gertrude, 'Look here, upon this picture, and on this.' Figure I: 10 is the exterior of a black-figure/red-figure cup, showing duels over fallen warriors being fought across the handles. On one side the warriors are in black-figure (dark on light), on the other side their opponents are in the new technique of red-figure (light on dark); between, the fallen black-figure warriors have their shields in red-figure. Across the front of the cup black-figure eyes and archers stand out from the light background, and across the back red-figure eyes and a trumpeter are highlighted against a background of jet and glossy black. The cup is signed by the potter Andokides. Some cups have the two techniques divided between interior tondo and exterior; and amphorae have back and front in different techniques (these are all now usually called 'bilinguals'; Cohen 1978). For whatever reason (Cohen 1989; Williams 1991a), whether a personal decision by one potter or painter (the Andokides Painter, Psiax, Nikosthenes?), or prompted by outside

Figure I: 10 Athenian 'bilingual' cup, from Chiusi, *c.* 520 BC. Diam. of bowl 53.5 cm.

influences (metal work, painted metopes), the new technique increases in importance as the century closes, and by 500 BC the most notable work in the Athenian pottery workshops is being carried out in red-figure (Boardman 1975a; Williams 1991a; Robertson 1992a). The thirty years from 530 to 500 BC were a most inventive period, with new shapes created and new experiments carried out; besides red-figure, there is white-ground (Sparkes 1991a: 98–100), coral red (Sparkes 1991a: 102–3), and Six technique (i.e. white figure; Grossman 1991) that applies added colour and incision on a black ground. Gradually the old technique dies out; it is still impressive until the close of the century with work from (for example) the Leagros Group, but only the traditional Panathenaic prize amphorae (Figures II: 16 (sixth century) and V: 4 (fifth century)) retained the old technique of black-figure beyond the middle of the fifth century (Beazley 1951/1986: chapter 8; Frel 1973).

This new technique gave the painters new challenges and new opportunities in their image-making. Euphronios, who is known as a vase-painter in the later sixth century and as a potter in the early fifth century, painted a scene (Figure II: 1) showing the lifting of the body of Sarpedon from the Trojan battlefield (the frieze is 20 cm (8 in.) deep). We can see that the figures are now drawn with a pen or brush, and there is an interest in the inner anatomical markings, in the spatial placing of the bodies, in the contrast between dead and living, in the fall of drapery. The body of the dead Sarpedon looks like an anatomical model for the students of surgery. The group of potters and vase-painters to which Euphronios belonged has in modern times been dubbed the Pioneers; they invented new shapes and gradually emancipated themselves from merely producing a reverse image of black-figure. Other major craftsmen are Phintias, rather old-fashioned, with a penchant for scenes of daily life (athletics and symposia), and Euthymides, an expert in creating realistic 3D poses. Some cup-painters are also known by name, for example Oltos and Epiktetos, but the number of unsigned vases, whether pot or cup, is much greater than the signed and of equal quality.

In the early fifth century, a generation after Euphronios and his contemporaries, the expressive possibilities of the technique were further developed, and corporeality was rendered with fewer markings, some major lines raised in black relief, others, less important, brushed on with a faint touch of pale brown. What had been spelled out muscle by muscle and fold by fold is now depicted with consummate ease and much less deliberation. As well as the popular stories from myth, subjects also include scenes of everyday life, both among the humbler artisans such as carpenters and metalworkers and at the sophisticated delights of an aristocratic drinking party: wine, women and music (cf. Figure III: 17). However, concentration on subject matter should not distract attention from the whole effect of the decorated cup. The early years of the fifth century, up to the time of the Persian Wars, are the acme of vase-painting when subject, composition and adaptation to shape were most in harmony. Vase and decoration are united, whether one is concerned with the larger pots or smaller cups. Of the painters of large pots (e.g. amphorae, kraters, hydriai), the painters who are known today by their modern names of the Kleophrades Painter who favoured heroic and divine subjects drawn with a powerful line (cf. Figures IV: 1 and 2), and the Berlin Painter who endowed his figures with grace (Figures IV: 4, 6 and 7), both learned from Euthymides. They can also both be shown to have painted black-figure Panathenaic prize amphorae (Beazley 1951/1986: 94–6/86–8; Matheson 1989). The cup painters, such as Onesimos (Figures IV: 9 and 10), the Brygos Painter (Figure II: 6), Douris and Makron, whose range of subject matter was very wide, were closer to Euphronios and most likely learnt from him. Potters' names are known in this period: Brygos, Python, Hieron, etc., as well as that of Euphronios himself.

Classical (*c.* 480–*c.* 300 BC): red-figure and white-ground

Later, after the Persian Wars, influences from the innovations that panel-painters such as Polygnotos and Mikon had introduced in Athens and Delphi had a deleterious effect on vase-painting (Robertson 1975: 240–70). The ground line was abandoned, and figures were set at varying levels; there were three-quarter views, overlapping, foreshortening and attempts at perspective. All were tried by painters in the early years, and all moved the craftsmanship of vase-decoration away from its proper channels (Boardman 1989a; Burn 1991a). Some traditionalists kept to the more well-trodden paths.

There were, however, compensations. A parallel technique to red-figure, that of white-ground, which also may have developed under the influence of panel-painting, shows the quality work that was being done in the years around 450 BC. On cups, with the interior surface covered in white, we see the effect – action is less insistent than before, as in Figure I: 11 where Apollo sits calmly pouring a libation. These were special commissions that are usually found in sanctuaries (Mertens 1974 – the Apollo was found appropriately at Delphi). Later in the century (from *c.* 460 BC to the end

Figure I: 11 Athenian white-ground cup, from Delphi, *c.* 470 BC. Diam. 17.8 cm.

Figure I: 12 Athenian white-ground lekythos, from Eretria, *c.* 440 BC.
Ht 42.5 cm.

of the century) the white-ground comes to be limited in general to use on
perfume containers (lekythoi) made for the tomb, with scenes that reflect
in different ways the connection with death – quiet scenes at home that
remind us of the life of the dead man or woman (Figure I: 12), or visits to
the tomb itself; scenes in the underworld and those that involve such figures
as Charon and Sleep and Death are also to be found (Beazley 1938/1989;
Kurtz 1975; Wehgartner 1983; Reilly 1989). The most notable painter

of white-ground lekythoi is the Achilles Painter, who is also a painter of red-figure (and of black-figure Panathenaic prize amphorae) and carries on the style of the Berlin Painter. The paint on these white-ground lekythoi is more fugitive than that on red-figure – they were made to be placed directly into the ground, and as the century progresses, the hard gloss outlines are replaced by dilute golden brown and then matt paint.

In the generation of the Parthenon (third quarter of the fifth century) some vase-painters mirror the Olympian stateliness that is a hallmark of the art of that time in Athens (Figure I: 13). Towards the end of the fifth century the figures in Athenian painted pottery tend more towards the sweet and mannered, with the ladies prettily posing, as it were for the camera. There is an increase in women's scenes, mainly wedding preparations, or in those mythological scenes where there is a notion of escapism and women are predominant (Burn 1987; 1991a and b), as in the story in which Herakles goes to the far west for the apples in the garden of the Hesperides, and the nymphs of evening gather the magic fruit for him; on the hydria by the Meidias Painter (Figure II: 13 (lower scene)) the nymphs posture before him like fashion models on the cat walk. The late fifth century is also characterised in Athenian painted pottery by a dazzlingly complex arrangement of figures set in vertical perspective and consequently lacking overall coherence (e.g. Figure V: 9).

Even before the outbreak of the Peloponnesian War in 431 BC, some Athenian potters and painters had emigrated to South Italy and Sicily (MacDonald 1981) and had successfully set up potteries of their own that catered for local markets, mainly pottery for the tomb, with scenes that concentrate on cult and myth. When the Athenians lost the war (MacDonald 1982), the western craftsmen who had grown up there and had learned their craft from the immigrant workmen took over the markets in the west. After a generation or so of settling down, by the fourth century centres (Mayo 1982; Trendall 1989; Padgett et al. 1993) have been distinguished in Lucania, Apulia, Campania, Paestum, and Sicily (Figure I: 14). Some workshops, particularly those in Apulia, produced brilliantly colourful effects and crowded compositions (Figure I: 15). Some of the Lucanian craftsmen follow in their wake but create less sophisticated compositions (Figure I: 16), and when the workshops move away from the urban centres, the style becomes even less refined. It is assumed that most of the market for these Greek pots were local Greeks, but the adaptation of some local, non-Greek shapes and the inclusion of native costume, as in Campanian (Figure I: 17), suggest a native market as well (Trendall 1971). There are two painters who add their names to their work in Paestan (As(s)teas (Figures I: 18 and V: 3) and Python) – a rare occurrence outside of Athens. Paestan also has a penchant for scenes from farce (Figure V: 3); whether the scenes are local or are adapted from stage productions of Athenian comedy is being argued (Taplin 1993).

Figure I: 13 Athenian red-figure volute-krater, from Spina, *c.* 430 BC.
Ht 77 cm.

By contrast, Athenian painted pottery of the fourth century has a more
uneven career (Boardman 1989a: 144–216; Lebel 1990). With the western
markets lost, the Athenians find an increased outlet for their products in
the Greek settlements in South Russia, and it is from the material found
there that the modern name Kerch is used to describe an output from

Figure I: 14 Sicilian red-figure skyphoid pyxis, *c.* 330 BC. Ht (as preserved) 29.2 cm.

Figure I: 15 Apulian red-figure lekythos, *c.* 350–340 BC. Ht 94.6 cm.

Figure I: 16 Lucanian red-figure volute-krater, *c.* 400–380 BC. Ht 51.3 cm.

Figure I: 17 Campanian red-figure hydria, said to be from Capua, *c.* 340–330 BC. Ht 59.7 cm.

Figure I: 18 Paestan red-figure calyx-krater, *c.* 360–350 BC. Ht 71.2 cm.

Figure I: 19 Athenian red-figure pelike, *c.* 330–320 BC. Ht 48.3 cm.

Athens in the mid-fourth century that is characterised by polychrome painting (white, yellow, blue, grey) with gilding and relief work (Figure I: 19). Although myth and everyday life are still the staple of the scenes, narrative is of less interest than the desire to pose the figures. By the latter part of the century production and quality are both limited. There are some other areas on the Greek mainland in which red-figure pottery was produced, such as Boeotia (Lullies 1940), Euboea (Gex and McPhee 1995), Corinth (Herbert 1977; McPhee 1983) and Laconia (McPhee 1986), but these centres never escape from the shadow of Athenian and are a pale imitation. Only Etruscan shows a beguiling originality (Padgett *et al.* 1993: 227–67; Boardman 1994a: 265–9). It may be noted that classical writers designate the fourth century as the great age of panel- and wall-painting (Pollitt 1990: 149–76); the vase-painters were obviously no match for them.

Figure I: 20 Athenian West Slope kantharos, from the Athenian Agora, *c.* 150–100 BC. Ht 23.6 cm.

Hellenistic (*c.* 300–*c.* 30 BC)

Painted pottery in the old technique of red-figure lasts only a little way into the Hellenistic period (Hayes 1991 for an overall picture). The painted decoration that is applied to the surface is now mainly added after firing (Athenian West Slope (Figure I: 20; Rotroff 1991), South Italian Gnathia (Padgett *et al.* 1993: 189–213), Canosan (Padgett *et al.* 1993: 218–19), Centuripe ware (Wintermeyer 1975; Padgett *et al.* 1993: 220–5), Hadra (Sparkes 1991a: 54–6), etc.), and the major output of figured pottery is that which is produced in relief moulds (Figure I: 21; Rotroff 1982; Sparkes 1991a: 109–10). Whatever ends the production of figure-decorated black-figure and red-figure ware served for over three hundred years, they are now served in other ways; new traditions were being established.

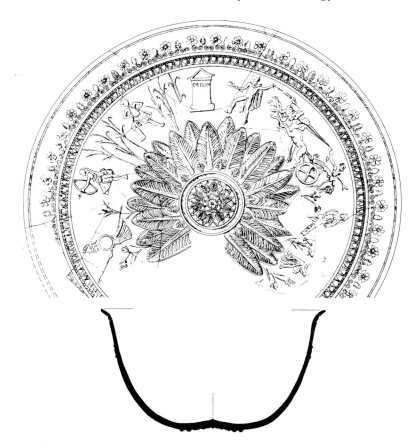

Figure I: 21 Athenian mouldmade bowl, from the Athenian Agora, *c.* 225–175 BC. Diam. 16.8 cm.

THE WIDER PICTURE

The brief summary just presented is, as it were, the picture-book view of Greek painted pottery. The development is seen partly from an art-historical and partly from an iconographic viewpoint with little or no reference to political or social background. This tends to be the traditional image conjured up for the casual observer, the museum visitor and the devotee of Greek art. The vases highlighted are usually quality pieces from the major centres with narrative scenes – the enticing 'lollipops'.

There will be more to say about the style and subject matter in Chapters IV and V. We have been drawn into looking at the vases as art objects;

they have an intrinsic attraction. This approach has been and still is aided by the attitude of some museums and the art market, the way in which a painted vase is treated as a status symbol, a mark of distinction and something collectable (see Chapter II). But at the time of their making they were not works of art in the modern sense, not objects to be admired in their own right.

Stress has recently been laid on the exceptional place that these 'lollipops' we have seen hold in the overall production of figured pottery. 'Potters were there primarily to provide cheap household ware for a wide public, and the bulk of ... black-figure and red-figure is just that, and has little or nothing to do with fine art' (Robertson 1985: 2). Indeed it has been queried to what extent 'art' has any place in the study of Greek pottery at all.

If we are intent on looking at Greek pottery from an art-historical viewpoint, then the majority of products will be seen to be of poor craftsmanship. One does not have to look far to see that a potter or a painter could be capable or incompetent, careful or careless, imaginative or dull, original or repetitive. Let one piece suffice to represent the thousands of Greek painted vases that in themselves do not deserve a second look by connoisseurs of fine work. Sometimes the painter has pretensions beyond his ability. One black-figure hack (Figure IV: 12) had the temerity to sign his work, and he did this round the edge of the vase with as little care as he executed his central scene: 'Oikopheles potted, Oikopheles painted me' – he even writes his name twice and uses the specific word 'potted' rather than the general word 'made' which is found in every other inscription! There are equal depths of ineptitude amongst red-figure painters (e.g. the Pithos Painter). We are on dangerous ground in treating Greek pottery, solely or even chiefly, from an art-historical point of view. It is a mistake to mix aesthetics with business.

Black and plain wares

But whether the quality of the figured and decorated pottery is good or bad, we are still swimming in a very small ceramic pond. Potters had other demands on their skill. Pots had functions, not necessarily active ones but functions nonetheless, whether domestic, sacred or funerary. So it is time to move out of the art-historical pool and set the painted vases in a wider context of production.

There was a vast issue of plain black vases in many different centres (Sparkes and Talcott 1970; Morel 1981; Hayes 1984; Sparkes 1991a: 103–10; Gill (forthcoming)). Some were produced in the same shops as the figured, others in centres that had no tradition of figured or decorated wares. Athens again was one of the major producers; later the centres are to be found in the various cities of southern and central Italy (Teano, Cales, Campania

Figure I: 22   Athenian black cup-skyphos, from the Athenian Agora,
c. 440–430 BC. Diam. 17.8 cm.

– see Hayes 1991). Recent study has brought them all more clearly into focus.

Figure I: 22 illustrates a black stemless cup made in Athens in the middle of the fifth century and carries a stamped pattern of leaves in the centre of the floor, most likely in imitation of metal work. Incised and stamped patterns are occasionally found in the centres of red-figure cups (Ure 1936 and 1944). There is a great variety of shapes in black, both open and closed: stemmed cups, jugs, oil flasks, small bowls, etc. The fourth century, both in Athens and elsewhere, sees some big shapes (hydriai, amphorae, kraters (Figure I: 23)) that carry ribbing and raised and gilded terracotta ornaments of wreath and necklace – these were for the tombs where often real gold wreathes and necklaces were laid (Kopcke 1964). Eventually it is this technique of all-black gloss with added colours and figures, and the shapes now often produced in a mould, that outlives the red-figure technique and becomes the hallmark of the Hellenistic period after Alexander (Figure I: 21; Rotroff 1982). The major producers of black wares in these later centuries are to be found in central Italy and further west (see e.g. Morel 1981; Hayes 1991; Sparkes 1991a: 103–9).

All that we have seen up to this point, both figured and black, have been what one might call table ware – fine wares of various grades: drinking

Figure I: 23 Campanian black calyx-krater, from Teano (Campania), *c.* 300 BC. Ht 64 cm.

cups, mixing bowls, oil flasks, whether for the living or for the dead. There are, however, other types of pottery – themselves wheel-made – that move us further away from the finer types. These were created to serve domestic or artisan needs, as for instance household basins (Figure III: 11), jugs, and mixing bowls, usually left plain on the outside but fully glazed inside to delay seepage and produce a smoother surface (Sparkes and Talcott 1970). There are also the heavy-duty pieces such as the Ali Baba jars, the pithoi, that were built on the spot and stood in the courtyard for the storage of household commodities, and their movable counterparts, the ubiquitous transport jars (Figure III: 16), the amphorae – jars for carrying wine, oil, fish, nuts, etc. These are long-distance containers, and it is possible to track the movements of their contents from their source across the Mediterranean and beyond (Peacock and Williams 1986).

Coarse wares

Still we have not exhausted the types of clay container. There is the coarse pottery made not on the wheel but by a paddle and anvil method – the shapes are thin in section, capable of being set on the fire or in the oven (Figures III: 2 and 10), and are the equivalent of kettles, casseroles, etc. (Sparkes and Talcott 1970: 34–6). There will be more to say and show of the potter's role in society in the third chapter when we shall return to the kitchen and to other rooms of the house.

The intention of this survey of the varieties of output has been to show that, when we are studying painted pottery with its figured scenes of myth and everyday life, we are looking at a small corner of a very large field. Painted pottery is not something that we should imagine in every household and used for every daily task (Osborne 1987: 108–12). There are indeed still difficulties over understanding what its role in the household really was.

It may now be easier to understand the meaning of the quotations with which we began ('great curse' and 'black hole'). Pots were made for a purpose and were painted for a purpose. The chocolate-box image of a Greek painted pot may suffice, and we may study it and respond to it on our own terms. But Greek vases (the word 'vase' has its own modern overtones today that we should not cast back to antiquity) were not art exhibits in the Greek world, to be appreciated for their intrinsic beauty, and for us a vase should be seen as an archaeological object that once had a context. The vases left the potteries to have a life in the orbit of a settlement, in the sanctity of a shrine, and in the embrace of a grave. They were not single items: they had functions, contexts, destinations near and far. They had a part to play in the social, economic and religious life of the Greek world. It has been asked in fact whether the study of Greek pottery is a subject in itself, should it not be discussed in a wider context altogether, have we not created a false picture by this emphasis on clay vases, an emphasis generated by a positivist approach.

BACKGROUND READING

Given the variety of approaches to the study of Greek pottery, any introductory book will tend to present its own partial view. Cook 1972 remains the basic handbook, but it provides a tough initiation; a new edition is in preparation. Williams 1985 (based on the British Museum collection), Sparkes 1991a (giving a broad view) and Rasmussen and Spivey 1991 (on various aspects) make entry into the subject easier. Of picture books, the best are Arias, Hirmer and Shefton 1962 (out of print) and Simon and Hirmer 1976/1981. Robertson 1959 treats only high-quality pieces and uses them to assist in understanding panel- and wall-painting.

Given the tendency to treat painted pottery as a category of art in its own right or as a means to appreciating other forms of art, it is usual to find painted pottery having a place in more general works on art, either in separate chapters or threaded into the history; for the former, see Richter 1987, chapter 11; Cook 1972/1976, chapter 2; for the latter, see Robertson 1975; Pedley 1992; Boardman 1993. For period studies, see Hurwit 1985 (Geometric and Archaic); Pollitt 1972 (Classical); Pollitt 1986 (Hellenistic); Charbonneaux, Martin and Villard 1971 (Archaic), 1973a (Classical) and 1973b (Hellenistic).

For the more detailed studies of specific centres of production in the Geometric, Orientalising and Archaic periods, see (for Geometric) Coldstream 1968 and Schweitzer 1971; (for Corinthian) Payne 1931 and 1933, and Amyx 1988; (for seventh-century Attic) S.P. Morris 1984; (for Boeotian) Kilinski 1990; (for Laconian) Stibbe 1972.

Athens needs a paragraph of its own. For black-figure, see Beazley 1951/1986 and Boardman 1974. For red-figure, see Boardman 1975a and 1989a, and Robertson 1992a. For white-ground, see Mertens 1974, Kurtz 1975 and Wehgartner 1983. For more detailed bibliography, see the background reading to Chapters IV and V.

For the South Italian centres, see Trendall 1989 with references to earlier, more detailed studies, mainly of his own. For Hellenistic, see Thompson 1934/1987; Green 1976; Rotroff 1982; Hayes 1991.

For black, plain and coarse wares, see Sparkes and Talcott 1970; for black, see Morel 1981, Miller 1993, Gill (forthcoming).

The *Corpus Vasorum Antiquorum* (*CVA*) series has been published intermittently from 1923. It is an international concern, publishing the ancient pottery that museums, both public and private, hold in different parts of the world. The emphasis has been, increasingly, on Greek figured pottery and, increasingly, on Athenian black- and red-figure vases. Quality, in text and illustrations, has inevitably varied, and equally inevitably the vases have been treated as individual items. For help through the complex structure, see Carpenter 1984b.

CHAPTER II

'COMMONLY CALLED ETRUSCAN VASES'

—— •◆• ——

At Sotheby's London auction rooms in December 1993 a collection of sixty-four Greek vases was sold for a total of five and a half million pounds, far outstripping the absurdly low estimates given in the sale catalogue (*Hirschmann* 1993). Three million pounds of that sum was paid for just two rare vases: a pair of Caeretan hydriai (Bloesch 1982: nos. 10 and 11; Hemelrijk 1984: nos. 29 and 25; *Hirschmann* 1993: lots 35 and 36; cf. Figure V: 5 for a Caeretan hydria). One alone fetched over two million – it is a perfectly preserved piece which on the front shows a hero, either Perseus or Herakles, fighting against a sea-monster and on the back a hunt after a stag and a goat. The prices paid for this and the other vases confirm, in one commentator's words, 'the continuing strength of the Greek vase market' (Eisenberg 1994: 30). Twenty years earlier the first 'million-dollar' vase was bought by the Metropolitan Museum of New York (von Bothmer 1976; 1981a): a red-figure Athenian calyx-krater (Figure II: 1) which displays a scene with the body of the Trojan ally Sarpedon being lifted from the field of battle by Sleep and Death in the presence of Hermes (cf. *Iliad* XVI.666–83). The vase bears the name of the painter: Euphronios, and of the potter: Euxitheos; the protagonists are also named, as is a young man of the day, Leagros, who is saluted as *kalos*, meaning 'handsome'. It is an excellently preserved and high-quality example of Late Archaic work, *c.* 510 BC.

These are two examples of one view of Greek pottery – that of the modern collector, whether private or public. Greek vases have been for some generations what are called in today's parlance 'collectables' – convenient in shape and size for museum or home, apt to be treated as isolated pieces, suitable for moving around in a display, and on occasion even presented as prizes to winners of TV quiz programmes. There is now a well-established academic tradition that enables unsigned vases to be stylistically attributed to painters both named and unnamed; the latter have names invented to distinguish them, and this procedure is sometimes extended to the naming of potters (see Chapter IV). The New York vase has the name of potter and painter written on the black of the background: Euxitheos and Euphronios; we have no names of the potters or painters of Caeretan hydriai, so all the names have been invented by modern scholarship. The hydria costing two million pounds has been attributed to a painter already designated as the Eagle Painter (Hemelrijk 1984: 45–6; for another

Figure II: 1 Athenian red-figure calyx-krater, *c.* 510 BC. Ht 45.7 cm.

hydria attributed to the same painter, see Figure V: 5); had it been known earlier, the painter might well have been dubbed the Seal Painter, after the entrancing creature at the left of the scene. Such invented names can be displayed in the sale catalogues and are no small incentive in raising the prices.

In order to understand why private collectors and museums are willing, not to say eager, to pay so much for a single vase, it is necessary to look at the history of the interest in Greek painted pottery (Cook 1972: 287–327) – whether we are looking for instances of academic curiosity or possessive greed, aesthetic pleasure or social cachet. It was not always so, and we need to see at what point in time the change took place, when Greek vases became collectors' items and when they engaged the interest of academics.

ANTIQUITY

We know that Greek pottery, even when large and decorated with figures, was cheap to produce and cheap to purchase (see Chapter VI). There is no evidence that clay vases were collected or studied in any serious way in antiquity. Naturally they may have evoked sentiment and pride, they were mended and laid as offerings for the dead in tombs, they were traded and distributed, but never ranked high in financial terms. The Roman élite, who collected so much Greek sculpture, seem not to have shown an equal interest in pottery. Literary references have been scoured in modern times for suggestions that the Romans valued pottery highly, and texts have been misinterpreted to produce the required meaning (Vickers 1987: 104–29; Vickers and Gill 1994: 1–32). It was customary at one time to single out an incident mentioned by the Greek geographer Strabo (b. 64 BC). In his *Geography* (Book VIII.6.23) he refers to the occasion when Corinth, having lain deserted for a century after Mummius' sack of 146 BC, was refounded by Julius Caesar in 44 BC. When the new settlers were clearing the ruins and digging open the graves, they came across bronze vessels and quantities of *ostrakina toreumata* – 'terracotta reliefs' (Payne 1931: 348–51). Admiration for these led to the ransacking of the graves and sale at high prices in Rome. Such clay *necrocorinthia* ('objects from Corinthian graves') flooded Rome for a time, but soon the supply dried up. Any possible connection of such pieces with what we call Corinthian pottery was abandoned by most scholars long ago. As Payne (1931: 348) remarked, 'it is surely difficult to imagine that archaic Corinthian vases would have won in Rome even such momentary popularity as Strabo describes: Rome rarely took much account of early archaic Greek art, and even more rarely showed any disposition to collect it'. It is possible that the *ostrakina toreumata* were Hellenistic relief vases – such as mould-made bowls (cf. Figure I: 21) or 'Plakettenvasen' (Dohrn 1985) – or maybe they were relief vases made with the help of clay moulds, the reliefs of which were taken from silver originals. Some instances have been unearthed now and again in modern excavations on the site of Corinth; some are of exquisite quality that might have caught the eye of Roman connoisseurs (Thompson 1949: 371–2). Of course, the question of what would suit Roman taste at the time has to be seriously considered.

At much the same time as the Corinth settlers were at work, those at the newly established colony at Capua, when demolishing some very old tombs (*vetustissima sepulcra*), found a quantity of vases of ancient workmanship (*aliquantum vasculorum operis antiqui*) and worked with more vigour as a consequence (Suetonius *Divus Iulius* 81). Whether these were Greek vases and whether the eagerness of the excavators was linked to a possible sale to collectors is not stated (Vickers and Gill 1994: 14).

MEDIEVAL AND RENAISSANCE

After the end of antiquity and before antiquarian interest in Greek pottery was aroused in Italy, it is not unlikely that some of those vases that had been distributed from Greece to Italy in antiquity had been unearthed by accident on Italian soil, more particularly from Etruscan tombs (de Grummond 1986: 21–6; Greenhalgh 1989: 236–8). Land clearance, drainage and the expansion of towns led to the accidental discovery of ancient pottery (Greenhalgh 1982: 7–9). The finder's reactions to his finds might not have been too sophisticated, as in some areas pots unearthed from the ground were for many centuries considered magic crocks that had been self-engendered or made by gnomes underground (Abramowicz 1978; Sklenář 1983: 16). But for us light does not begin to dawn until the late Middle Ages, and even then it is reflected and distorted, not direct, light. We find written references that may make mention of painted pottery, but these are rare and open to various interpretations. It may be preferable to look at the art of the later Medieval and early Renaissance periods to catch a reflected glimpse of lost influences.

Let us look at the evidence century by century, starting with an example selected from the early thirteenth. Figure II: 2a shows Bonaventura Berlinghieri's panel-painting which presents the St Francis cycle; it is to be found in the fourteenth-century church of San Francesco at Pescia near Lucca. The painting itself dates from AD 1235. It has been noted that in many of the vignettes that surround the central figure of the saint (e.g. Figure II: 2b), the artist has used an unusual floral palmette pattern as an architectural frieze on the wall. It was suggested by Ernst Gombrich (Gombrich 1976) that the artist had accidentally encountered a Greek vase, maybe a piece which we today would designate fourth-century Apulian (see Chapter I), had been attracted by the design and incorporated the floral pattern into the various scenes of his panel. If this is so, it would be a rare example of the post-antique use of Greek pottery and an early indication that Greek pottery was being found and was being noticed by artists, if not by scholars. This particular suggestion has not received universal approval; other scholars would rather derive the inspiration for this wall decoration from terracotta or stone architectural friezes (Greenhalgh 1989: 237–8). Later in the same century Ristoro d'Arezzo mentions vases that have recently been claimed to be not only Roman Arretine ware (as is usually thought) but also black-figure and/or red-figure (Harari 1988: 70, n. 2).

Let us move to the fourteenth century. Sixty years ago Fritz Saxl (Saxl 1957: 151) pointed out that some fourteenth-century frescoes from a private house in Venice (now in the Museo Correr) may have interest for those seeking visual evidence for the influence of Greek pottery. The main figures are the three Virtues (Figure II: 3a). We are not concerned with those; it

Figure II: 2a Panel-painting of the St Francis cycle, in Pescia, AD 1235.

Figure II: 2b Detail of Figure II: 2a.

Figure II: 3a Wall-painting of the Virtues, from a house in Venice, fourteenth century AD.

Figure II: 3b Detail of Figure II: 3a.

Figure II: 4 Corinthian pyxis, from South Russia (?), early sixth
century BC. Ht 16 cm.

is the small figures on the tops of the gables that are worth noting: they
are all virtually naked and the right hand figure (Figure II: 3b) bends
forward and looks over the back of his hand – 'a most un-mediaeval
attitude' commented Saxl, who suggested a sixth-century BC Greek *komos*
figure from Corinthian pottery (e.g. Figure II: 4; see Seeberg 1971) as the
inspiration, concluding that 'where this trecento painter expresses himself
without feeling restricted by church rules, he uses the classical model'.

When we reach the fifteenth and sixteenth centuries, in view of the
heightened interest in antiquity that artists, craftsmen and scholars were
beginning to show, the modern hunt for reflections of figures taken from
Greek painted pottery becomes more earnest. Here are some examples of
the sort of evidence that has been thought to indicate knowledge and use
of Greek painted vases at this time.

For the first example we move to the fifteenth century. In the 1460s
Piero della Francesca was painting frescoes in the church of San Francesco
in Arezzo. In the apse he painted the Legend of the True Cross and began
his story in the upper right lunette with the Death of Adam (Figure II: 5).

Figure II: 5 Wall-painting of the death of Adam by Piero della Francesca, in Arezzo, AD 1452–66.

It has been suggested (Vickers 1985–6: 156) that the head of old Adam shows the influence of a Greek red-figure vase-painting; as a parallel an Athenian cup of *c.* 480 BC, found in Vulci in the nineteenth century, has been cited (Figure II: 6). The head of Adam with white hair and pointed beard has been compared with the head of old Phoenix, Achilles' tutor, and other details may support a connection. It is interesting that at exactly this time (1466) we have our first detailed description of an Etruscan tomb being excavated, though certainly not the first to be opened (Greenhalgh 1982: 20; de Grummond 1986: 25–6).

A second suggested dependence dates from the same time. Whilst Piero della Francesca was at work in Arezzo, the painter Pollaiuolo was also working in the 1460s, painting frescoes in the Villa della Gallina at Arcetri, near Florence. As long ago as 1920, a proposal was put forward (Shapley 1920) that the light on dark figures, the sense of movement and the emphasis on line to create form recalled Athenian red-figure, and further evidence has recently been added to back up the suggestion (Vickers 1977; cf. Fusco 1979; Greenhalgh 1982: 17–19). The vases that come closest in comparison

Figure II: 6 Athenian red-figure cup, from Vulci, c. 480 BC.
Diam. 32.5 cm.

are those of the second quarter of the fifth century – a satyr scene from a volute-krater found in a tomb excavated at Spina south of Venice in the 1920s and dating from c. 460 BC (Vickers 1977: figure 8; cf. figures 4–7) has been used to indicate the sort of vase and scene that could have supplied the source. (Naturally neither the Vulci cup nor the Spina krater are the specific sources of influence.) One tomb in Tuscany, or even one multi-figured vase from such a tomb, could provide all the necessary details. Again not all scholars are convinced that the connection provided the impetus; some suggest that it may be coincidence (Ettlinger 1978: 145–6; Weiss 1969: 189, n. 7). Other suggestions have been made for the possible influence of vase-paintings on painters and sculptors, for example Giotto (Greenhalgh 1982: 45–6) and Donatello's Cantoria and the doors of San Lorenzo (Greenhalgh 1982: 98–103, 114–15).

Again in the later fifteenth century we read of experiments to reproduce the lost process of colouring vases in terracotta, red and black. This information comes from Vasari's *Lives* (Vasari 1991: 393–6); he gives a brief account of the life of his great-grandfather, Lazzaro Vasari (1380–1452), and comments that it was his son Giorgio (1416–84) who was interested in old Arretine vases of terracotta ('il quale attese continuamente all'antiquità de'vasi di terra aretini') and made large vases on a potter's wheel. He also presented four excavated vases to Lorenzo de' Medici who seems to have had a preoccupation with pottery (see below).

The soil of Italy was not the sole provider of Greek vases. The Turkish control of the eastern Mediterranean naturally did not put a stop to all contact between East and West. Not much later than the period we have been considering, we read that in 1491 Lorenzo de' Medici was offered for his collection three Greek terracotta vases that had recently been brought from Greece to Venice, and the letter that announced their arrival also suggests that they were not the first to enter his collection (Vickers 1977: 187; Yuen 1979; Greenhalgh 1982: 18; 1989: 237). So it seems that Greek vases were being collected, and we may have two visual instances as confirmation of this.

For the first instance we enter St Augustine's study as visualised by Carpaccio (Figure II: 7) in a fresco of the early sixteenth century painted for the Scuola di San Giorgio degli Schiavoni in Venice (Lauts 1962: 230–4; Greenhalgh 1982: 17–18; Lyons 1992: 1). It has been characterised as 'the picture of an ideal Venetian museum' ('la représentation d'un musée idéal vénetien', Wasbinski 1968: 26), and attention has been drawn to the left side of the painting. It is full of detail, and there is a shelf of objects that

Figure II: 7 The vision of St Augustine by Carpaccio, in Venice, AD 1502.

has been claimed to include Greek vases – maybe a small stamnos and a skyphos or lekanis lid. If St Augustine, as has been suggested, is indeed a portrait of the Greek bishop, Cardinal Bessarion, who settled in Italy and more than once was nearly elected pope (Reynolds and Wilson 1991: 149–52), and to whom the Scuola was indebted for a special indulgence in 1464, then there may be a reference to his Greek background. But we should not allow ourselves to be carried away, for then the question arises – did the painter know these were Greek vases, and if so, how? That painted pottery was reaching Venice from the eastern Mediterranean is clear from the incident of Lorenzo de' Medici mentioned above.

Another, slightly later view of Greek pots on a shelf may be seen in a pen-and-ink sketch by Lorenzo Lotto of 1526 (Figure II: 8; Rykwert 1980: 273). Perhaps we may here be a little more certain that what we are looking at are indeed illustrations of Greek pottery; one shape closely resembles a tall Greek lekythos. Again we may turn to the contemporary written evidence – a generation later (1565) a Spanish engineer working at Orbetello accidentally fell into an Etruscan tomb and discovered figured vases (Vermeule 1958: 203, n. 33; Cook 1972: 287).

All these examples are suggestions of influence, and all have been denied by one scholar or another. They are all noted in connection with artists

Figure II: 8 Pen and ink drawing of a cleric in his study by Lorenzo Lotto, AD 1526–7.

and the influence the objects may have had on them. Only these last two (by Carpaccio and Lorenzo Lotto), alongside a few literary references, indicate any sort of collection, and none of the major collections shows much interest in Greek pottery – after all, terracotta vases could not compare with the sculptures or gems and cameos (such as the 'Tazza Farnese'), nor with the silver and the gold objects that the Medici and others collected. However, I have mentioned the imported Greek vases that were being offered to Lorenzo de' Medici, so he was not totally averse to their charms. One would also like to know whether at much the same time the vase that Livia, the ladylove of the poet Fausto Andrelini, broke, was Greek or not. The poet calls it painted and 'alexandrian' (whatever he meant by that designation) and describes the figures on it: Ganymede, and the gods, and the Judgement of Paris. 'Liviam vehementer increpat quod cyathum variis historiis depictum fregerit' ('he scolded Livia violently for breaking a cup painted with various stories'), but all ended happily when he consoled her: 'deinde eam solatur' (Saxl 1940–1: 39; Weiss 1969: 185).

SEVENTEENTH AND EIGHTEENTH CENTURIES

There still exists a good number of sketchbooks of the fifteenth and sixteenth centuries in which artists recorded their versions of classical architecture and sculpture, but these are always compiled in a random way, as an *aide-mémoire* for future work (see e.g. Bober and Rubinstein 1986). We enter a new stage in our understanding and our evidence when we come into contact with Cassiano dal Pozzo's Paper Museum. The splendid exhibition mounted at the British Museum in 1993 highlighted the interest that was starting to grow in the seventeenth century for this much more systematic collection of drawings of classical antiquities; dal Pozzo sent artists, Poussin included, to draw the antiquities of Rome (Turner 1993). The collection of drawings (which of course comprised more than classical antiquities) is now scattered, and much research is being carried out to try and rebuild it. Although the main emphasis in the classical section centred on all known sculptures in the Rome area (from 1620 onwards), drawings of the minor arts are also evident and, amongst them, vases. These have been described (rather heavy-handedly but correctly) as 'the earliest recorded examples of post-Renaissance graphic consciousness of Greek or South Italian painted vases' (Vermeule 1958: 203). The drawings were not published at the time, and it has only been since the late nineteenth century that interest has been shown in them, an interest that has quickened in the last few years. The drawings are mainly to be found in Windsor Castle and the British Museum. Here (Figure II: 9) we have a (lost) bell-krater treated as a painted vase – vases are beginning to be seen for themselves, not simply as ammunition for other art. We now know that it was made in Apulia in

Figure II: 9 Drawing of an Apulian bell-krater from the dal Pozzo album, *c.* AD 1640.

the fourth century (see Chapter I) and shows a popular composition of youth and woman in conversation. It is a large drawing – 45.8 cm × 35.8 cm (15 in. × 12 in.) – in pen and brown ink with a yellow and black wash, and is dated to *c.* AD 1640. It has been described as 'one of the earliest accurate and sympathetic renderings of such a vase' and it is noted that 'the drawing is sufficiently good to allow the vase to be attributed to a specific group of vase-painters, the circle of the Eton-Nika Painter' (Bailey 1992: 19). But some drawings were not so fine and are, in Robert Cook's words, 'of an improbable crudity and carelessness' (Cook 1972: 290).

There is a quickening of interest in the seventeenth century, and although there are only a few references to the collecting of vases it may have been more prevalent than is usually assumed; vases were not yet illustrations of wealth nor subjects for catalogue publication, so they rarely receive a mention. But in the seventeenth century there was a change in attitude towards vases: they were less frequently grouped with natural objects as articles fit for cabinets of curiosities, and were more seriously treated as objects in their own right. Before the close of the century one or two vases had actually been published, for example in de la Chausse's *Romanum Museum* of 1690 (von Bothmer 1987: 185; Lyons 1992: 2), and it has been noted that it is material from South Italy and Sicily that is most prominent, with excavations at Capua, Nola and elsewhere. But it is of course the eighteenth century that marks the beginning of a more widespread interest in Greek painted pottery. The vases were becoming more plentiful and were collected more widely.

Despite the preponderance of South Italian vases, an Etruscan origin for pottery (alluded to in the title of this chapter 'commonly called Etruscan vases') was strongly canvassed, partly through the publication of Dempster's *de Etruria regali* in 1726 (Leighton and Castelino 1990). This work, written a century earlier, was motivated by political prejudice and played on local pride, and at the time of publication transferred a popular notion into a more scholarly view (Vickers 1987: 115; von Bothmer 1987: 188; Lyons 1992: 2). The origin of Greek pottery in Etruria was upheld by the majority of antiquarians in the more northerly parts of Italy, not because they would have recognised an Etruscan vase, if one had magically risen, like the crocks mentioned above (p. 37), fully grown from the ground in front of their eyes, but because antiquarian Etruscophilia was dominant amongst Roman and Tuscan scholars, and examples of painted pottery had indeed been found in Tuscany. At that time Tuscan patriotism was of more importance than scholarship, and the notion of pottery being traded from Greece itself in antiquity was not seriously contemplated. The Etruscophiles could of course claim that the vases found in South Italy were unearthed in lands that were once under Etruscan control. This would allow an extension down to the bay of Naples and beyond.

In the eagerness of scholars to back up their ascriptions, ancient literary sources were inevitably brought into play. If the text did not fit the theory, the text could be counted corrupt; after all, were not scribes prone to error? To take the best known example, in Pliny the Elder's *Natural History* (XXXV.160), a work much consulted at the time, the manuscript has the phrase 'maior pars hominum terrenis utitur vasis' – 'the greater part of mankind uses clay vases'. It was suggested that the word 'terrenis' was corrupt and should read 'Tyrrhenis' ('Etruscan'). Philology ruled.

But it was Naples that was a major centre for antiquarians, and there were some private collections that contained their full share of vases. The Valletta collection has been seen as a major one, and its sale in 1766 has been pronounced

a turning point in the history of vase collecting and vase studies . . . [which] heralded the interdependence of connoisseurs and scholars, the market and the academic establishment. The development of a market in which pottery acquired significant monetary value coincides precisely with the period of mounting scholarly recognition.

(Lyons 1992: 3)

A second collection was sold in 1766, that of the Marchese Felice Maria Mastrilli, and a recent study (Lyons 1992) of a manuscript entitled *Spiega de' vasi antichi* (now in the Resources Collections of the Getty Centre for the History of Art and the Humanities) has thrown much light on the Neapolitan scene in the middle of the eighteenth century. The manuscript, dated *c.* 1755, includes essays and careful, if tutorless, illustrations (e.g. Figure II: 10; see Lyons 1992: 17, with n. 75 for the use to which this particular vase was put). The text and illustrations give technical details (e.g. the colour and quality of the clay) and precise measurements, and are an early example of the organising of a body of material. The text also shows that the collection was displayed in a manner that was in advance of its time (cf. Jenkins 1988): no longer were the vases treated as curiosities; they were historical documents and art objects. The range of vases purchased by Mastrilli reveals that he had catholic taste: most of the important Greek wares made in the Italian regions were represented in his collection, and he favoured 'pretty' vases that had subjects which lent themselves to antiquarian study of themes and functions (religious rituals, marriage, sacrifice, etc.). Some of the scenes were 'improved' with overpainting, either to enhance their interest or to conceal their perceived immorality.

The inscriptions on the vases led to a change in the notion of an Etruscan origin. By the middle of the eighteenth century, although the Etruscan position was still strong and would continue so in the popular imagination, a Greek origin for painted pottery had already been canvassed. In 1745 Sebastiano Paoli noted (see Lyons 1992: 18): 'on those [vases] which are called Etruscan and which with greater reason might be named Campanian . . . Greek letters appear quite frequently, Etruscan letters more rarely'. The Greek lettering of the inscriptions in the background of the painted scenes was beginning to make scholars think again. In 1754 A.S. Mazzocchi studied six inscribed vases; he read the Greek in the background and came to the right conclusions: the vases were made and painted by Greeks (von Bothmer 1987: 187; Lyons 1992: 5, 17–18). If an origin in Greece itself was hard to contemplate, there was the much nearer old 'colonial' territory of South Italy and Sicily where Greeks had started to settle from the eighth century BC onwards. Finds were being made rather more frequently there than in the north. Indeed, the red-figure vases studied by Mazzocchi had come from old Greek cities of South Italy (Nola, Sant'Agata dei Goti), so they were considered to have been made in Greek South Italy. On the premise that pottery was made near to where it was found, they had the stronger case.

Figure II: 10 Drawing of an Athenian pelike, once in the Mastrilli collection, *c.* AD 1755.

It was in the dying days of the Etruscan theory that Josiah Wedgwood and his partner Bentley named their new Ornamental Works in Staffordshire 'Etruria', and it was in Etruria, England, on 13 June 1769, that the 'first-day' black pots were turned out, to be decorated later in London with red caustic enamel – a far cry from the technique of the original decoration (Vickers 1987; Vickers and Gill 1994: 20–2). But by this time the study, understanding and marketing of ancient painted pottery was entering a new and important phase. Indeed, Wedgwood had based some of his designs (including those of the 'first-day' pots) on the plates of a set of volumes that were soon to be published and of which he had seen proof copies (Rykwert 1980: 403, n. 12); they had in large measure given him the impetus to his new venture. We are here of course entering on more familiar territory.

In 1764 there had been appointed as 'his Britannick Majesty's Envoy Extraordinary and Plenipotentiary at the court of Naples' a man who holds a prominent place in the history of the study of Greek pottery. Sir William Hamilton (1730–1803), who was in his mid-thirties at the time of his appointment, was a man of many interests, but he 'loved two things in particular, Greek vases and volcanoes; living in Naples [as he did from 1764 to 1800], he was luckily able to enjoy them both' (Tillyard 1923: 1). The 1777 portrait of him from the school of Joshua Reynolds in the National Portrait Gallery in London shows him with some vases at his side and the volumes of his magnificent new publication on his lap and at his feet – and there is smouldering Vesuvius to be glimpsed low down in the background: sheer bliss (Fothergill 1969; Burn 1987: plate 1b). As early as 1766 he had amassed a collection of vases. This he did by buying from local antiquarians such as Porcinari and Mastrilli (mentioned earlier) or by clandestine excavations in the surrounding countryside. He is said to have 'created a market that emptied many Neapolitan drawing rooms, drove up the prices and spurred vigorous, although often illicit, excavation' (Lyons 1992: 4; cf. Ramage 1990; for Hamilton's opinions on excavation, see Ramage 1992).

Hamilton did not purchase the Mastrilli collection in its entirety; he was not attracted to the 'pretty' vases but preferred the simpler compositions and styles, and the less flamboyant themes. It was these he bought, and in so doing laid his enormous influence on the future development of the neo-classical movement, of which Wedgwood's pottery was an early beneficiary.

His influence arose because he decided to sell what he had acquired, and to this end set about publishing a sale catalogue of his collection, with a dedication to George III. His first four volumes which were published in Naples from the late 1760s onwards were entitled *Collection of Etruscan, Greek and Roman Antiquities from the Cabinet of the Honourable William Hamilton*. The vases were, in the words of the text which accompanied the plates, a collection 'equally proper for the compleating of well understood

Collections of Prints and Designs, or to furnish in a manner not only agreeable but useful and instructive, the Cabinet of a Man of Taste and letters' (d'Hancarville 1766–7: 168). This set of volumes was one of the first important and scholarly works on the subject; it was sumptuously produced, with coloured drawings of the figured scenes (Figure II: 11), squared off with a decorative border and with diagrams of the shapes on separate plates, and on occasion with updated versions of the compositions.

The text was to have been written by Winckelmann who in 1764 had published his *Geschichte der Kunst des Altertums* (*History of Ancient Art*) and had studied and appreciated Greek vases. However, the association came to nothing: Winckelmann was dead by 1768, and Hamilton turned to the self-styled Baron d'Hancarville (Haskell 1987: 30–45). Now here was a very shady character! It was said of him (Figure II: 12) that 'His penetrating, voracious eyes, his flaring nostrils, his lips which barely touch each other are the outward signs of his longing to see everything, he wins you over with his learning and his prolific and imaginative way of speaking' (Haskell 1987: 30). That was his effect on a woman, the society hostess Isabella Albrizzi. However, Sir Horace Mann wrote to Walpole of d'Hancarville as 'a strange man [with talents] that only want common honesty to make him a brilliant figure' (Haskell 1987: 38). It has recently been shown (Vickers 1987; Vickers and Gill 1994: 6–14) how cleverly, and

Figure II: 11 Drawing of an Athenian calyx-krater, from near Gela, once in the Hamilton collection, AD 1766.

XIV

Figure II: 12 Pen portrait of d'Hancarville.

d' Hancarville

Figure II: 13 Athenian red-figure hydria, late fifth century. Ht 52.2 cm.

indeed wilfully, d'Hancarville misinterpreted the ancient literary evidence to enhance the (supposed) value that clay vases had in antiquity. He claimed that they were made by the best artists of the day, each potter producing only a few vases: 'he did less but he did better'; but one has to admit that d'Hancarville did say that the vases were of Greek manufacture, even if the workshops were located in Campania itself. Thus he was able to set high the asking price of the collection that Hamilton had put together. Even the order in which the vases were published, and in which the different sections of the text were arranged to appear, has been seen as a clever selling gambit, to increase interest and enthusiasm to purchase. It is also noted that the volumes were published at a time when porcelain was highly prized (indeed one of the main factories was the Royal Neapolitan Factory in Naples itself), and so the false arguments of the value of ancient pottery fell on receptive ears and eyes. Some of Hamilton's vase pictures were used as decoration on the porcelain, produced in Naples, Sèvres and Berlin (e.g. Figures II: 10 and 11) – so the mixed effect was able to profit both products (Govi 1992). Even so, compared with fine procelain, the Greek vases were comparatively inexpensive (Lyons 1992: 23, n. 30), but certainly far in excess

Figure II: 14 Caricature of Lord Nelson by Gillray. AD 1801.

of their original price. It was also the time when elegant simplicity, as Wedgwood learned to his advantage, was replacing the fripperies of rococo.

Indeed, the earliest painted portrait which incorporates a vase rather than a fragment of statuary is that of Ferdinand, Duke of Brunswick and Lüneburg, painted by Pompeo Batoni in 1767 – exactly at this time (Greifenhagen 1939: plates 1–3; Jenkins 1988: 449–50). Painted pottery had started to become a fashionable adjunct and status symbol.

The best known of the vases published in the first set of volumes was the Meidias hydria (d'Hancarville 1766–7: plates 127–30; pp. 166–8; now British Museum E 224; Burn 1987: 1–2). We know it as an Athenian red-figure hydria of the late fifth century (Figure II: 13); we also know that it carries the name of the potter Meidias, and hence today the painter, whose name is not known, is called the Meidias Painter, but the inscription was not noticed until 1839, seventy years after the publication. Winckelmann saw the vase and pronounced it, in a characteristic outburst of hyperbole, 'the finest and most beautiful drawing in the world' ('allervortrefflichste mit der schönsten und reizendsten Zeichnung der Welt', Eiselein 1825: XI.449). It was indeed the jewel in the Hamilton crown and later became notorious because of the caricature made from it by James Gillray (Williams 1985: 54, figure 60). Gillray shaped it into the outline of Admiral Lord Nelson (Figure II: 14), who by the end of the eighteenth century had moved in to take up residence in Hamilton's household as the lover of Hamilton's second wife, the celebrated Emma. The caption below proclaims: 'From Sir William Hamilton's Collection'.

The sales pitch was successful. Hamilton somehow managed to bypass the law banning export of antiquities from the kingdom of the Two Sicilies (Lyons 1992: 6–7), and in 1772 the British Parliament bought the collection for the vast sum of 8,000 guineas (£9,600). The road to the five million pound sale of December 1993 was open. Even Goethe was affected: we read in his *Italian Journey* his entry for 9 March 1787 when he was in Naples:

> Large sums are currently being paid for Etruscan [NB] vases and, to be sure, you can find some beautiful and exceptional pieces among them. Every foreigner wants to possess one. You grow less cautious with your money here than you would be at home. I am afraid that I myself will be tempted.
>
> (trans. Auden and Mayer 1970: 196–7)

Two years later, in 1789, Hamilton was building another collection and took part in excavations at nearby Nola, 'the richest source for Attic vases until the discovery of the Etruscan necropoleis of Vulci, Tarquinia and Cerveteri' (Lyons 1992: 9; cf. Lezzi-Hafter *et al.* 1980). The frontispiece of his second set of publications shows him (at the age of 60) with Emma at Nola, and he is delicately holding a newly found krater

(Greifenhagen 1963: figures 2–3; Williams 1985: figure 1). One might be tempted to say that he knew how to handle a vase better than he knew how to handle Emma. Publication began again, on a slightly less lavish scale than before. This time the draughtsman was William Tischbein, a friend of Goethe's, who had been appointed Director of the Academy of Paintings in Naples.

The title of the new volumes was *Collection of Engravings from Ancient Vases mostly of Pure Greek Workmanship Discovered in Sepulchres in the Kingdom of the Two Sicilies* (Tischbein 1791–5). The introduction to the volumes stressed the Greek origin of the pieces and recognised the Athenian nature of much of the subject matter. As has been pointed out, Hamilton selected for purchase from earlier collectors the less elaborately decorated vases, and in this way was influential in forming a taste for Athenian vases at the expense of South Italian (Lyons 1992: 15). He claimed that his second collection was finer than his first and made arrangements for the material to be shipped to England. The main bulk of the packages travelled in the 'Foudroyant' and reached England safely; a third of them were packed in the ill-fated man-o'war the 'Colossus' which on 10 December 1798 sank off the Scillies. The wreck was located off Samsun in 1974, and experts from the British Museum had the interesting task of identifying and piecing together the fragments recovered (about 30,000) with the help of the drawings which had been published almost two hundred years earlier (Morris 1979; 1984). It is like having the black and white pictures on the lid of hundreds of jigsaw puzzle boxes, and most of the coloured pieces missing from inside.

NINETEENTH CENTURY

By the beginning of the nineteenth century the amount of material known was becoming greater than before. A watercolour of 1798 shows an art dealer's shop in Naples (Greifenhagen 1963: 89, figure 5; Knight 1990: 37, figure; Lyons 1992: 4); Hamilton himself may be one of the buyers. Naples was the centre of the art market and the shelves display the wares, with shapes completely restored, where necessary, on the same principle as the classical sculpture of the time, and the painted scenes touched up or completely redrawn, as had become normal practice. Scholars devised various schemes for sorting out the different techniques, origins and styles, but no system was really possible yet. Also, no method of dating had yet been devised, as in the matter of chronology no help could be derived from ancient authors, and the interpretation of the subject matter of the scenes, and attempts to connect them with events in Greek and Roman history, brought confusion in their wake. Subjects that were concerned with Dionysos, which were noticed as being popular, tended to be erroneously attached to the Roman decree of 186 BC concerning the worshippers of Bacchus, as this was the best known event linked with the god reported in Latin texts (Livy XXXIX.14.3–18.9; *CIL* I.196). Interpretation was in general faulty and overdone, and a prey to mystic extremes.

Certainly, interpretation of the subject matter was the major concern. It was some time before style was considered, though *c.* 1800 the discovery of an amphora at Agrigento pointed the way (von Bothmer and Milne 1947; *Agrigento* 1988: cat. no. 59). The subjects are on one side Theseus killing the Minotaur and on the other the weighing of goods (Figure II: 15), but the vase also carried the name of a Greek maker – Taleides, the first to have been observed (you will recall that the Meidias inscription was not read until later). We now know that the Taleides amphora was made in Athens *c.* 540 BC; not surprisingly at the time of its discovery it was considered to be Sicilian Greek. But major attention was not yet turned to style or painters.

Figure II: 15 Athenian black-figure amphora, from Agrigento, *c.* 540 BC. Ht 29.5 cm.

The late eighteenth and early nineteenth centuries saw the more expansive unfolding of Greece and the eastern Mediterranean. In 1805 the painter Edward Dodwell, on his second journey in Greece, bought a lidded bowl in Corinth, now known as the Dodwell pyxis, and it was rightly considered to have been manufactured near the find spot (Amyx 1988: 205–6, plate 86). In 1813 Thomas Burgon, an English merchant resident in Smyrna, was present in Athens when a grave containing a Panathenaic prize amphora (Figure II: 16) was exposed; inside the amphora were some small and plain vases, along with the cremated bones (Corbett 1960: 52–8; Williams 1985: figure 34). The contents were published in 1822, and in a letter to a friend about the find in 1831 Burgon is at pains to stress the circumstances of the find, the genuineness of the pottery and especially of the inscription on the amphora:

> as the recent discovery of so many Panathenaic prize-amphorae in Italy, with inscriptions analogous to that on mine, has given rise to discussions, in some of which the genuineness of my Vase (especially its inscription) has been called into question, it becomes necessary for

Figure II: 16 Athenian black-figure Panathenaic prize amphora, from Athens, *c.* 560 BC. Ht 61.5 cm.

me to state that I washed and joined the fragments myself, with the greatest care, in Athens. The Vase was never out of my possession, and has not been *restored*, in the Italian sense of the word; the inscription is, therefore, in every respect genuine . . .

(quoted in Corbett 1960: 53)

Greek vases found on Greek soil were beginning to show the justice of the Greek claim, but the struggle was still in some cases uphill and a prey to academic dispute.

As he indicated, Burgon had reason to fear for his good name, as in the late 1820s excavations had begun at Vulci. The year 1828 was the *annus mirabilis*, and in the following year the international Instituto di Corrispondenza Archeologica was established in Rome (von Bothmer 1987: 189–92). It was through the reports published in the organs of the Institute, the *Bullettino*, the *Annali* and the *Monumenti*, that the findings from the excavations conducted by Edouard Gerhard, the Institute's founder, were made known and fully described. Excavation is a dignified name for the pillage and plunder that took place then. The site sixty miles north-west of Rome was on land that mostly belonged to Lucien Buonaparte, the Prince of Canino, brother of Napoleon. He was a tricky customer, and the Princess was no less so (for a drawing of the family group, see Ansaldi 1937: 563, figure 3; Sforzini 1989: 70, figure). Plain pottery was stamped upon by the workmen on the orders of the overseer (de Grummond 1986: 42; Small 1994: 43, n. 52). As George Dennis commented when he was present in the 1840s at the opening of one particular tomb (note his perceptive remark 'valuable as relics of the olden time'):

> Coarse pottery of unfigured, and even of unvarnished ware, and a variety of small articles in black clay, were its only produce; but our astonishment was only equalled by our indignation when we saw the labourers dash them to the ground as they drew them forth, and crush them beneath their feet as things 'cheaper than seaweed'. In vain I pleaded to save some from destruction; for, though of no marketable worth, they were often of curious and elegant forms, and valuable as relics of the olden time, not to be replaced; but no, it was all *roba di sciocchezza* – 'foolish stuff' – the *capo* was inexorable; his orders were to destroy immediately whatever was of no pecuniary value, and he could not allow me to carry away one of these relics which he so despised.
>
> (1907: I.432)

Such behaviour was intended to enhance the value of figured vases, of which 3,000 had been unearthed by the end of 1829, mainly Athenian black-figure, red-figure and white-ground (de Angelis 1990).

Inscriptions, including names of potters and painters, were now relatively plentiful; thirty names were found in one year, to join the only one known before. But there was no systematic digging, few contexts were noted, vases found together were not kept together. It was treasure hunting. Because of the developments in the study of Greek vases that had begun in the previous century, the view now was that excavated vases were instant treasure, and they were soon put up for auction by Gerhard. Why the cemetery of a small Etruscan town should produce such a wealth of high quality painted pottery is still not clear. In fact any modern publication of Athenian black-figure and red-figure is likely to be unbalanced by the number and quality of the vases from Vulci (see here Figures I: 6; II; 6, 17; IV: 2, 5; V: 1, 2, 6, 8; in addition the famous black-figure amphora with Achilles and Ajax dicing, and signed by Exekias as potter and painter, was found there at this time, and among non-Athenian the Laconian black-figure cup with King Arcesilas of Cyrene; see de Angelis 1990: 45–50). As Dennis remarks with regard to the Princess's property (1907: I.431, cf. Vickers 1987: 125; Vickers and Gill 1994: 23):

> And a pretty property it is, rendering a large percentage to its possessor; for while her neighbours are contenting themselves with well-stocked granaries, or overflowing wine-presses, the Princess to her earlier is adding a latter harvest – the one of metaphorical, the other of literal gold, or of articles convertible into that metal. Yet, in gathering in the latter harvest, the other is not forgotten, for to lose no surface that can be sown with grain, the graves, when rifled, are re-filled with earth. On this account, excavations are carried forward only in winter.

Such a harvest of pottery on Etruscan soil inevitably raised the question of origin again – you recall Burgon's protestations about his truthful account of the Athenian find: Panathenaic prize amphorae had been found at Vulci. But the Prince of Canino was minded to dismiss or belittle the evidence from Greece:

> [W]e ask, which is most probable, that the Etrurians, lords of the sea and of Italy and of the Islands, should have introduced one or two of their fine vases into Greece; or that the Greeks, who have never spoken a word of masterly paintings on earthen vases, should have brought to our Hypogea thousands of them, which in the first ages of Rome were already buried, or that Greek artists should have come to paint master-pieces in Etruria, which they never painted at home?
>
> (Canino 1831: 267–8)

It is fine rhetoric, if poor logic – the Prince was proud of his findings:

> This single discovery of ancient Italy suffices to show that not only the fine arts, and the imagination that produces them, but that the sciences, and the meditation from which they spring, were the

property of our Peninsula, when Greece was still barbarous, and the remainder of the west in darkness.

(Canino 1831: 265)

So after all, in the Prince's view, that old, popular ascription was correct: the vases were indeed made and painted in Etruria, and of course were highly valuable.

Interpretation was still struggling to find its way. Take one example from Vulci (Boardman 1987a: 141–3): the well-known Athenian black-figure cup signed by Exekias as potter (Figure II: 17). The interior shows Dionysos sailing in a boat on a wine-dark coral-red sea. His vine-stalk, with its branches and grape clusters, twines round the mast. The reference is most likely to Dionysos' capture by pirates whom he changed into dolphins

Figure II: 17 Athenian black-figure cup, from Vulci, *c.* 540 BC. Diam. 30.5 cm.

(*Homeric Hymn VII*) – here they circle the ship. At the time of discovery in 1829, one interpretation was that the scene showed Noah's ark, an interpretation abetted by a misunderstanding of some marks on the outside surface of the vase. It was thought that there were demotic Egyptian, Phoenician or Hebrew letters to be deciphered here; we now know that they were merely cracks on the surface of the black gloss. However, once astray, the chariot of misinterpretation plunged recklessly in the wrong direction, and the perfectly legible signature 'Exekias made' was understood to refer to Hezekiah. So it would be a mistake to entertain any ideas that the flood of new material immediately produced answers to all questions. In fact, at that time scholars would not really have known what it was that needed questioning.

Some artists of the nineteenth century were drawn to the shapes and designs of Greek pottery, and with the gradual increase in the popularity of classical subjects it is perhaps not surprising to find that both figures and shapes of pots gain a place in the canvasses of the time. Influence has been seen in the work of David and Ingres (Greenhalgh 1978: 214), and later in the nineteenth century the 'Olympian Dreamers', such as Lord Leighton, Watts and Alma-Tadema, mix adaptations of classical sculpture with references to vases (Wood 1983; Jenkins 1983a; 1988).

As the century progressed, the academic passion for interpretation subsided. Those European museums that had benefited from the sale of vases from Vulci and other sites in Tuscany such as the Campana material from Cerveteri (von Bothmer 1977) – museums in London, Munich, Paris, Berlin, the Vatican – had material to display, in chauvinistic fashion, even if it was not always made readily available to the general public. The view of Greek pottery at this time was proprietary, and one has the feeling that the continuous closure of some public museums today has this same proprietorial air about it. Close study of the exhibits was considered unwarranted voyeurism, and the desire to take notes in front of the objects an example of unjustifiable inquisitiveness. We know that J.D. Beazley, when visiting museums in the early years of this century, found his study hampered in this way. As Dietrich von Bothmer explains:

> On [his] first visits to the Villa Giulia, note-taking was strictly forbidden, and Beazley had to leave the galleries and go outside the museum every time he wanted to jot down what he had just seen and remembered. He became so good at this practice of committing to memory what he could not write down in front of the object, that towards the end of his first study trip to Rome, he did not have to leave the museum after every vase that he had absorbed, but could recall correctly between eight to ten vases before dashing out to write up his notes.
>
> (von Bothmer 1985b: 10)

The nineteenth century saw the beginning of the second phase in what has recently been designated (Orton, Tyers and Vince 1993: 4) as a three-phase development in the study of ceramics (art-historical; typological; contextual). Museum curators had the task of bringing order into the hundreds of vases in their care and of taking note of the new finds that were now, with increased excavation in the eastern Mediterranean, filling the shelves of local storerooms. Otto Jahn produced his *Beschreibung* of 1854 (Jahn 1854), a description of the Munich collection. This work is usually singled out as the first of the professional catalogues that later curators took as their pattern, and it is the work which some recent scholars have seen as the beginning of a dark age of systematisation and separatism that must now be undone (Hoffmann 1979: 63–5). Jahn shunned symbolic interpretation and went for factual 'objective' recording: shape, technique, context, subject matter, date. Analysis of style – connoisseurship – was only just starting to make headway. Greater distinction was being made between shapes, and there was more accurate drawing of the scenes. In some cases photography was introduced, and stylistic observation started to become more precise. Adolf Furtwängler's *Berlin Katalog* of 1885 (Furtwängler 1885), which acknowledged the divisions by fabric, period and shape, as had Jahn, also paid attention to style and stylistic affinity, and thus was inaugurated what has been termed the 'century of attribution' (von Bothmer 1987: 197; cf. Kurtz 1985b: 238).

The most influential figure in this area of research has been J.D. Beazley, who was born in 1885, the year that Furtwängler's catalogue was published. He worked ceaselessly for over sixty years at ordering and attributing thousands of vases and fragments (Kurtz 1985b). His friend, Bernard Ashmole (1970/1985: 448/61), recalled that 'even on [his] wedding day he was allowed after a time to go to the Ashmolean [Museum], whilst [his wife Marie] continued to entertain the guests'. (For his work, see Chapter IV.)

A century is a long time in scholarship for one view of a subject to hold centre stage. The art-historical tradition that has been dominant this century has in a way highjacked the material, and the connoisseurship approach to vases and their painters has accentuated the cheque-book mentality that is fed by the tomb robbers of Tuscany and the dealers in the art-market capitals of the world (on looting and the antiquities market, see recently Cannon-Brookes 1994; Isler-Kerenyi 1994). This view will doubtless continue to be strong, as the commentator I quoted at the beginning indicated (p. 34). But there is an academic tide that is turning against it. Greek painted pottery was a popular product, it was for everyman, and it is right that it should not be left wholly in the hands of the art lover or viewed as a trophy behind glass or made the object of auction-house bidding. It is salutary that Greek vases, the elaborate figured pieces as well as the more mundane coarse pots, are increasingly being viewed in the context of those aspects of Greek life – society, religious ceremony, funerary ritual, economics and trade – that brought them into being.

BACKGROUND READING

For a brief but full statement of the history of the study of Greek vase-painting, the best treatment is Cook 1972: 287–327 (based in part on Jahn 1854). More recent work is to be found in Hoffmann 1979; von Bothmer 1977; 1987. An important article which makes clearer the early eighteenth-century developments that preceded Hamilton is Lyons 1992; see also Vickers 1987 and Vickers and Gill 1994: chapter 1. Knight 1990 presents a well-illustrated account of Naples in the time of Hamilton.

For studies that look more widely at the influence of classical art on Western art and include Greek vases, see Rowland 1963; Vermeule 1964; Greenhalgh 1978; 1982; 1989; Haskell and Penny 1981.

CHAPTER III

'WATCHED POTS'

——— •◆• ———

INTRODUCTION

The last chapter showed how for historical reasons Greek vases – painted with figures, floral and geometric decoration – began to be studied, and to some extent are still studied, primarily as art objects. 'Art' is a dangerous word, especially if it is art with a capital A and especially if used of pottery, as it can conjure up such diverse images: today if the subject is pottery as art, one is likely to think in terms of Bernard Leach or Lucie Rie. 'Art' earlier meant 'craft', an acquired skill, not necessarily related to painting or sculpture (the 'fine arts', as we might still call them and linked with aesthetics (see Taylor *et al*. 1994)). The English poet, John Milton, could refer to the Italian astronomer and experimental philosopher Galileo as 'the Tuscan artist'. We derive our word art from the Latin 'ars'; when we go back to the Greek language, we meet a word that takes us nearer to the older idea we need in connection with pottery: 'technē' – skill, technical ability, craftsmanship. The Greeks had no separate word for art – each maker displayed his own 'technē', whether he be blacksmith, cook, metalworker, sculptor, potter or painter.

Modern museums place a heavy emphasis on art as beautiful objects to admire – and rightly so. To be given a chance to gaze at a painting or sculpture by a great artist is a pleasure that we all seize eagerly. But museum curators have a tendency to treat all objects in their care as treasure in this aesthetic sense, and even those objects that in their own day served mundane functions and made no pretensions to be high art have these days become art by metamorphosis, art by transfer (Malraux 1978). Nonetheless, the role that a museum, even a museum of art, has in teaching about past societies, involves it in much more than aesthetics.

A prime example of this art by transfer is Greek pottery. Because some of the black-figure and red-figure vases are undeniably beautiful to our eyes and because many are now highly priced collectables (see Chapter II), Greek vases have over the last two hundred years come to be considered as Greek treasure, despite the fact that the aspect of the pottery that concerned its monetary value was relatively unimportant in antiquity. Indeed, the overemphasis on this aspect does injustice to the potter and painter, and unbalances the whole picture of form, use, purpose, context, technique, etc. And of course museums have been, and in some cases still are, fed with

64

their new acquisitions from archaeological contexts – indeed over the past centuries all museum artefacts have been removed from sites – whether settlements, sanctuaries or cemeteries.

Greek potters, whether working seasonally within the family or in a more industrial setting, were not free agents fashioning speculative pieces; they were business men who had a job to do, a living to earn, and a market to meet. They produced pottery to serve functional ends, and had to complete any commission they had been given. Deadlines were as important then as now: some festivals needed prize containers, so dates had to be noted during the year; the grape harvest demanded its annual ration of equipment, including crockery, so the potter had to be ready to supply it; the sailing season must not be missed if the ships were to carry the potter's goods overseas; etc. The potters had to have an eye on the clients and consumers, that is on all those consuming Greek pottery. So, in this chapter we shall not be concerned with aesthetics, nor with painters and styles, nor with the matters of iconography and iconology (see Chapters IV and V). We shall concentrate on more down-to-earth matters than taste and connoisseurship.

The evidence on which we base our understanding of pottery production falls into four categories (Sparkes 1991a: 2–3). First, we can study the vases themselves, and investigate them for their techniques of manufacture (Noble 1966/1988) and for the residues that they may still contain (Jones 1986: 839–47). Second, we can study the workshops, as some kilns have been excavated that enable the processes and the organisation to be better understood (Jones 1986: *passim*; Sparkes 1991a: 8–13). There are, thirdly, a few, mainly unhelpful, literary references that have survived (Richter 1923: 82–105). And lastly, images of potters and painters at work, mainly on Athenian black-figure and red-figure vases (e.g. Figure III: 1), can be seen as subjects of the scenes on the vases (Beazley 1944/1989: 88–98/39–47); Ziomecki 1975: 23–7, 147–57; Seeberg 1994; cf. Himmelmann 1994: 23–48). The Greek potter was a craftsman who had the skill to produce shapes to meet all the needs of life and death. And what this chapter will do is to take an aerial view, as it were, of various social contexts and walks of life, to see what demand there was for the potter's skill and how the potter, and the painter, responded to it. This is Greek pottery from the consumers' point of view. The examples are taken mainly from sixth- and fifth-century Athenian products, but they have wider application.

As mentioned earlier, modern study has tended to concentrate on Greek pottery that is decorated with figured scenes – the 'artistic' pieces in the modern meaning. The figured scenes are useful in enlarging our understanding of the contexts in which household and other objects were used, but this does not entail the assumption that the shapes depicted were necessarily of clay, much less of figured ware. It is true that some are shown broken, so presumably intended to be clay, and some have figures painted

Figure III: 1 Athenian red-figure bell-krater, *c.* 430 BC. Diam. 37.6 cm.

on them (cf. Figure III: 4), but these should not seduce us into thinking that all others were the same. The figured pots are only a small percentage of the output of workers in clay (for the tiny percentage that have survived, see Oakley 1992: 198–200), and they raise particular problems of use.

Manual dexterity with clay was needed for all types of work. The various potteries issued a huge range of products: clay was one of the fundamental resources of the ancient Greek world, and one has only to think of such products as the sun-dried and baked bricks that were used in wall construction, the terracotta roof-tiles of public and private buildings, and underground water-pipes that might form part of a Greek city's water system, to begin to realise the vast range of uses made of clay, whether baked or unbaked. Different potteries doubtless had different specialisations; for instance, it is unlikely that brick and tile works also issued painted pottery. Clay statuettes, whether hollow as perfume pots in the shape of humans, animals or birds, or solid little figurines for toys: these may have been made in factories especially devoted to them, but whether this is so or not, within the range of pot production the need for different varieties of clay container was immense. There were the gritty pots (Figure III: 2), some of which would be set over the fire; they are lightweight and thin (Sparkes and Talcott 1970: 32–43). Then there were the heavy duty 'Ali

Figure III: 2 Coarse hydria and kados, from the Athenian Agora, c. 575–550 BC and c. 500 BC. Ht of hydria 39.2 cm.

Baba' pithoi that are still made nowadays in different areas of Greece in much the same shapes as in antiquity (Schäfer 1957; for pithos-making in recent years, see Hampe and Winter 1962). There were also plain household bowls and jugs, and black gloss fine wares (e.g. Figure I: 22; Sparkes and Talcott 1970: 9–34), right on to the upper end of the market – with magnificent painted mixing bowls and wine jars, and elegant cups and jugs (Figures *passim*; Arias, Hirmer and Shefton 1962; Simon and Hirmer 1976/1981).

The potter's craft came not only in producing 'beautiful' objects like these last; the potter was mainly skilful in fashioning shapes that suited the purpose or purposes for which they were required – he would have soon been out of a job if he did not. This of course gave the potters a wide choice, and popular shapes, whilst retaining a basically similar form, changed over the years in proportion and details (cf. Richter and Milne 1935; Kanowski 1984). It is these changes that enable modern students of Greek vases to plot the course of their development, though it must be said that it is easier to do this with fine wares than with others, as the changes tend to be more overt and detailed. So here we shall be concerned with use in general and in particular: what purpose the shapes served, what needs dictated their production, what occasions called forth the potter's skill.

Most contexts of life needed the potter, and it will be possible to see for what purposes customers and clients, buyers and consumers visited the pottery shops in which the wares were sold, or for what reason the potters took their latest products to the nearby markets. Attention will be focused on local use; this is not the occasion to consider distribution further afield (see Chapter VI). This is Athens as seen from the point of view of pottery demand.

DEATH

The start will be made not with life but with death and its rituals (see I. Morris 1992). It is the graves in all those parts of the classical world that Greek pottery reached that have produced most material, particularly figured pottery. In Athens the main potters' quarter, the Kerameikos (i.e. the ceramic area), was situated near the main cemetery – it lay just outside the north-west gate of the classical city wall, in the low-lying area by the stream of the Eridanos that provided some excellent clay beds. Considering the heat and the difficulties of refrigeration, the need to dispose of the dead was paramount; there must have been a brisk, not to say urgent, demand for all sorts of funerary furnishings. The consequence of this is that grave goods, to borrow a clothing analogy, will have been 'off-the-peg' and not 'bespoke'.

Pottery played an important role at the lying-in-state and the mourning, and vases were required at the graveside ritual at the time of death and burial (Kurtz and Boardman 1971). There was also the custom of burying clay pots with or by the dead, and sometimes the provision of a clay coffin as a container for the unburnt body and the offerings. If the body was cremated, not inhumed, then the potters might provide a rather more elegant container, different shapes of amphora and ash urns, to house the cremated remains. Add to this the bringing of offerings, often perfume pots, to the graveside later, as an act of remembrance, and it is obvious that pottery production for the funeral trade was virtually never-ending.

Because of the protection that burial underground provided, it is the graves that have furnished decorated pots still in their unbroken, or if broken, their complete state, whether from the Geometric, Orientalising, Archaic or Classical periods (e.g. Figures I: 1, 2, 6, 12, 13; cf. Kurtz 1984). This has tended to emphasise the importance of grave material in modern study and highlight the position of figured pottery in society in general.

In the fifth century in Athens the most easily recognisable funerary vase for oil is the tall white-ground oil flask – a shape we call today the lekythos (Figure I: 12; see Beazley 1938/1989: 26–38; Kurtz 1975), and it may be that the Greeks called it by that name too (identifying the ancient names of the pots is a tricky business). Great care was lavished on some of the lekythoi; they could be technically complex, and in certain cases there was a small, inner container below the neck that held only a small amount of perfumed oil, what one might call a token thimbleful only (Noble 1966/1988: 24–5/66–8). It has been suggested that the outer, visible container was created to allow the painter a wide area for his composition, even when the amount of oil offered was small. Quality vase-painters decorated the white surface with scenes that speak directly to us of sadness and separation. The tombstone on occasion acts as a gloomy backdrop to brooding figures of dead men seated on the steps of their tombs, their friends and relatives around them; the emotional register is sometimes very sombre. Other scenes mix the living and the dead in the context of the home, or present life after death with Hermes, Charon, etc., and make reference to death through mythological paradigms.

Of course, it was the contents that were important, no matter whether in large or small amounts. Oil was a vital element in funerary ritual – for anointing the body itself, for including amongst the grave goods, to sweeten the atmosphere, and for placing on the steps of the grave at various fixed occasions of memorial in the months that followed death and burial. Not every oil container was so grand as the white-ground lekythos; some were obviously much more cheaply made, and the decoration on the small and squat pieces, often only a few inches high, is often very perfunctory, whether in black- or red-figure technique, with floral designs or hastily daubed figures, or plain black (cf. Figure VI: 1). The potter had to cater for all levels of society – and customers were provided with what they could afford. It does not mean that the anguish felt by the family was any less real because of their inability to purchase the more expensive products. Funerary offerings in the Archaic period and earlier were more munificent than those in the later periods; as time went by, less expense was lavished on the dead.

Some graves were furnished with a great range of shapes – a funerary 'set', as it were (for the difficulty with the words 'set' and 'service', see Small 1994: 41–3): containers for oil, mugs and cups to drink from, and even small cooking pots. Your needs in the next world or on your way there might be varied. The Kerameikos cemetery has provided some elaborate groups, as one from an offering ditch by a woman's grave of the late fifth century (Figure III: 3; Knigge 1991: 145–7). In this group there is a single white-ground lekythos, and some of the smaller and cheaper types of lekythos on the right; then some lidded bowls and caskets, associated with the life of Athenian women; plates and bowls; and a large water jar. Towering over the others are two rather ungainly ceremonial 'wedding bowls', lebetes gamikoi. Not all the funerary 'set' was necessarily made for the grave; in some cases the wear and tear on the vases and the mends that they have undergone show that they were used in life before being consigned to the tomb.

Figure III: 3 Vases from an offering ditch in a grave precinct, from Athens, Kerameikos Cemetery, late fifth century BC.

WOMAN'S WORLD

Let us now move from the grave to the lives of women (whether mothers and babies, brides or daughters) and see the importance that pottery had for them. The women of Athens made their own particular demands on the potteries. In fifth-century Athens the life of honest women, whether married or single, was severely circumscribed to the home (see e.g. Cameron and Kuhrt 1983/1993; Fantham *et al.* 1994; Blundell 1995). The houses usually faced inwards to a central courtyard, and there were few windows from which the ladies of the house could be seen from the street. It was in the home that the virtue of a young girl would be carefully guarded. A move from her father's authority and care to that of her husband would give her little more freedom than she had had before (Oakley and Sinos 1993). Some vase pictures show the wedding procession on foot, the bride signified by a veil over her head. On such occasions music was played on the lyre, and torches were lit at the end of the day to light the way forward to the bride's new home, sometimes represented by a column and door (e.g. Boardman 1974: figure 77).

The wedding itself would mean business for the potter; as with funerals, weddings demanded their range of vases. A pair of vases similar to the tall, lidded pair seen amongst the grave goods (Figure III: 3) can also be glimpsed in the context of the (surprisingly leisurely) wedding preparations (Figure III: 4). This is the famous Alcestis scene (the object that carries the scene will be mentioned later). Alcestis' name is written in the background along with those of her friends such as Theo, Doris, Hippolyte, Asterope and so forth, and on the other side (not shown) are personifications (Shapiro 1993) such as Hebe (Youth), Peitho (Persuasion), Himeros (Desire), Harmonia, and Aphrodite herself with her winged son, Eros. The bride may be named on the object as Alcestis, the self-sacrificing wife of Admetos in the legend who agreed to die in her husband's place – but she is any Athenian bride preparing for her wedding day. If the new bride received this object as a present, she would no doubt be reminded of her duty to be as good a wife to her husband as the heroine was to hers. If, as is possible, the object was made specifically for the grave (see below), there is a double irony in that the girl may have died unmarried and again differ from Alcestis in that for her there was no return to life. One friend is shown thrusting twigs into vases of the shape seen earlier, while another is arranging branches in a tall ceremonial vase at the centre of the composition; this is the nearest we approach to Greek vases for flowers, but the actions had a religious significance in the context of the wedding. All three vases in the scene carry sketchily painted figures on them in black. Related to the vases shown, there was also a slightly different shape, tall with elongated neck: the loutrophoros, which often carried scenes of the wedding

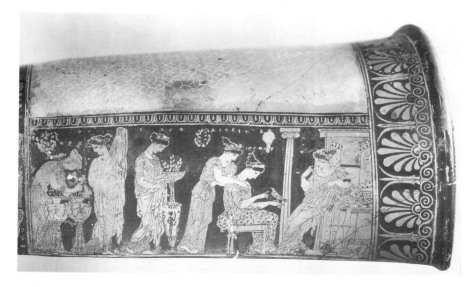

Figure III: 4 Athenian red-figure onos, from Eretria, *c.* 430 BC. Length 29 cm.

procession; but it was not for the wedding, it was placed at the graves of those who had died unmarried (Oakley and Sinos 1993), as indeed the Alcestis article may have been. The loutrophoros could be even more elongated than the stemmed wedding bowl – certainly rather ungainly to handle, and the shape must have been a test of a potter's skill in shaping his material as well as an indication of the strength of the Athenian clay itself. It is likely that the wedding vases would have been buried with the woman, whether married or not, or may have been specially made to accompany the woman to her grave (Reilly 1989).

Other containers that the potter might be asked to supply for the wedding day were various shapes of lidded bowl. One such was what is today called a lekanis (Figure III: 3, far left at the back), but we cannot be sure whether the Greeks would have used the same word. It was often highly decorated on the flat lid and useful for holding trinkets, jewellery and cosmetics; some were less elaborately embellished, and the black gloss is perhaps intended to have the brilliant radiance of silver. Another lidded bowl was what we call a pyxis (Roberts 1978; this is not very likely to have been the Greek word, for the word simply means 'box'). The shape is also to be seen on Figure III: 3 (third from the left at the back). Again the potter showed his skill, as bowls and lids are notoriously hard to make fit together, and some were marked with letters incised on both bowl and lid before firing, to make sure that they could be matched when taken from the kiln after the firing was completed. Some of the smaller bowls were used for powder. The figured lekanides and pyxides often carried scenes of weddings and home life, but also, like the Alcestis scene, might display scenes that had reference to stories of love and romance. The story of the Judgement of Paris was a suitable subject to decorate a vase that had a marriage context, even if it is a story that, as with Alcestis, is seen more from the man's point of view than from the point of view of the bride herself.

Perfume for the ladies was another commodity that needed a container. On Figure III: 5 one scene shows a girl holding out a narrow bottle to be filled from the jar of oil on the ground (a lekythos is shown hanging between them), on the other scene the same girl (?) presents the bottle to a seated woman at home (indicated by the mirror in the background and the basket on the floor). The perfume-seller is likely to be a slave woman from the cut of her hair. The bottle is what was known as an alabastron – most likely its proper name. On Figure III: 6 are two examples of the same shape with a black jar like the one that is at the feet of the two women on Figure III: 5a. But these alabastra are not made of clay, they are made of alabaster itself (a type of limestone/gypsum); potters were quick to borrow the shape, produce imitations of it in clay, and paint them white – an alternative that could be made locally and manufactured more cheaply than the carved stone versions. Business is business, after all.

a

b

Figure III: 5 Athenian
red-figure pelike,
c. 470–460 BC. Ht 27.3 cm.

Figure III: 6   Black pelike, alabaster alabastron and funnels, from the
Athenian Agora, fifth century BC and Hellenistic period.
Ht of pelike 26.6 cm.

Lekythoi might sometimes be made as wedding presents – in pairs. A
well-known pair, now in New York, have contrasting scenes. The first
(Boardman 1974: figure 77; von Bothmer 1985a: cat. no. 47) served to
remind the bride of her wedding day and of the procession to her new
home. The donkey- and mule-drawn carts approach the house, one with
the wedded pair and best man, another for important male guests. One
woman walks along by the donkeys with torches, followed by three others
who accompany the carts; the groom's mother, already in the house, holds
a torch and raises her hand in greeting. The second lekythos of the pair
(Boardman 1974: figure 78; von Bothmer 1985a: cat. no. 48) is the same
shape. This scene would remind the bride of one of her future tasks as
mistress of the household – supervising the wool-working and cloth-making
(Figure III: 7): the weighing of the wool, the making of the roves, the
spinning with the spindle, the weaving at the upright loom with the vertical
threads held firm by the loom-weights just above the ground, and finally
the folding of the finished cloth. In this area of home production, the
potter's services would be needed as well (Figure III: 8) – for such mundane
but necessary equipment as the heavy loom-weights, fastened to the bottom
of the vertical strands in order to maintain the tension of the warp threads
on the loom. There were also the dainty, decorated spindle whorls to weight
the spindle on its descent from the spinster's hand; these too could be made

Figure III: 7 Athenian black-figure lekythos, c. 550–540 BC. Ht of vase 17.1 cm.

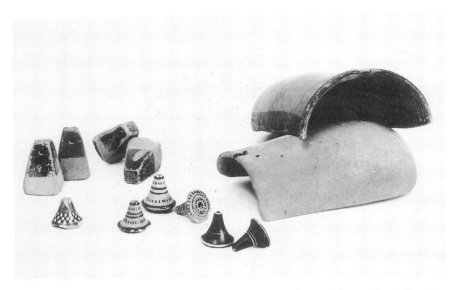

Figure III: 8 Spindle whorls, loom weights and onoi, from the Athenian Agora, sixth and fifth centuries BC. Length (of onoi) 23.7 and 28 cm.

of clay. There were also the knee-guards (onoi or epinetra), bulky objects that look like split drain pipes, about a foot long, and that fitted over the knee of the women as they untangled the wool. Sometimes the objects were fashioned with a head for decoration at the closed end and with raised scales designed to catch the pieces of dirt and grit that still clung to the unspun wool as it was pulled across the thigh. It is not a very attractive object, though the elaborate Alcestis scene we saw earlier was painted on one such – but it was an object over which many an Athenian women would have toiled. A graffito on an Athenian black-figure cup announces that the cup was a prize for wool-working (Milne 1945), but there are unlikely to have been many prizes for the women's daily tasks.

Babies would soon follow the marriage, or parents would want to know the reason why – annually in some cases, boys for preference. The breast seems to have sufficed to an alarmingly advanced age, but safer that than any other method of supply. Eventually there would have to be a visit to the potter's shop. The baby would require a feeding cup, and then later the family would need to buy a child's potty in which to install and train the growing infant. The one that still survives (Thompson 1971: figure 40) is a sturdily built object. Babies obviously needed the sort of encouragement or distraction provided on some vases by competent Athenian mothers (Figure III: 9). The potter would be more than willing to supply toys, dolls

Figure III: 9 Athenian white-ground cup, from Athens, *c.* 460 BC.
Diam. of cup 12.7 cm.

and rattles to amuse the children (Klein 1932; Rühfel 1984; Jenkins 1986),
as he would be eager to provide the small jugs (choes) that carried scenes of
small children at play and have been connected by modern scholars with the
festival of the Anthesteria (van Hoorn 1951; cf. Hamilton 1992).

The housewife would also need to carry out or supervise the other household tasks and eventually pass on her knowledge to her growing daughters.
We have already seen her at her spinning and weaving duties. Cooking
then, as now, needed a whole battery of utensils, and although some of
them may have been of bronze, many were clay, and households would
obtain a range of kitchen wares such as these ancient equivalents of kettles
(Figure III: 10) – not perhaps as aesthetically pleasing as the finer wares
but demanding skill on the part of the potter (Sparkes 1962 and 1965;
Sparkes and Talcott 1970: 224–6). The kettles and buckets were not made
on a wheel as were the figured vases which would never have been set on
the fire; they were shaped by hand with a paddle and anvil, to produce a
thin texture that is fire-resistant. There were barrel cookers used for baking
(Sparkes and Talcott 1970: 233; cf. Sparkes 1962: 137, no. 79; 1965: 163,
no. 79A) – the lumps of dough were slapped on the inside of the barrel,

Figure III: 10 Coarse kettles, from the Athenian Agora, sixth to fourth
centuries BC. Ht of largest 25 cm.

and on a fragment of a red-figured scene one can see smoke and flame
emerging from the stoke hole at the bottom (Sparkes 1981). One woman
in the scene may be bringing more dough in a handy-sized bowl; this was
an all-purpose container, waterproofed with black gloss inside and decorated with a black stripe or two outside (Figure III: 11). This type of bowl
makes an appearance in other contexts.

The buckets (Figure III: 2, right) were shaped for a specific purpose – they
were for use at the well that many houses would have had in their courtyard
or at the back of the house. On Figure III: 12 a woman holds a bucket over
a well-head, and in her right hand she flourishes the well-rope and hook that
fit over the bail handle across the mouth of the bucket. The well-head itself
was made of clay, a product, like so much else, of the potters' shops, whether
in the shape of the top of a pithos ('Ali Baba' jar) or with a more cylindrical
shape with strengthened, horizontal lip on which to rest the bucket. There
were often two holes on opposing sides to take a bar of wood against which
the rope would run free. Buckets were also made of bronze.

Wives and daughters of citizens went out rarely; there were religious
festivals in which they would sometimes have an important part to play
(Fantham *et al.* 1994: 83–96; Blundell 1995: chapter 14), but it was the slave
girls who more often would be sent out on everyday errands (Williams
1983b/1993), frequently to the fountain for water. This was the occasion
for the hydria or water-jar to be used (Figure III: 2, left) with its vertical
handle at the back for carrying when empty and the two horizontal handles
at the sides for lifting when full. Some examples were of coarse fabric

Figure III: 11 Plain lekanai with stripes, from the Athenian Agora, late sixth and early fifth centuries BC. Ht of larger 22 cm.

Figure III: 12 Athenian red-figure cup, *c.* 480 BC. Diam. of picture 12 cm.

(Sparkes and Talcott 1970: 200–1), not wheel-made like the figured pottery; indeed it is doubtful whether we should ever imagine the figured water-jars being employed in this way at all (Dunkley 1935–6; Diehl 1964; Manfrini-Aragno 1992). They were fancy versions that did not serve the useful functions of the everyday rough-and-tumble of the struggle at the fountain for water. The work-a-day water-pots were either of rough, lightweight fabric or of metal.

Within the house clay lamps were lit in the evenings – humble but necessary articles and needing above all to be functional (Howland 1958; Bailey 1963 and 1975; Perlsweig 1964). We can trace their development from the seventh century onwards. Some of the fifth-century pieces are so similar in detail and gloss to the black pots of the time that they were most likely made in the same potteries as the vases. Lamps would have been a steady line of business, if not very lucrative; they were exceedingly cheap (Gill 1987). On Figure III: 13 there is the intrusion of the male into the women's world. He is no doubt drunk, as he brandishes the torch with which he has found his way home in the middle of the night – if this is his own home and not some unofficial stop on the way. He is using the butt end of his torch to beat at the door. Behind the door a woman, small lamp held in her left hand, tentatively approaches, finger brought up to her lip. This is surely the wife at home, and not some lady of the night eager to receive a caller into her world. Note the painter's attempts at a roof – here the tiles remind us of another area of the clay-worker's craft.

SANCTUARIES

The finds that have been made in the excavations of sanctuaries (Bremmer 1994: 27–37), whether on the Acropolis of Athens (see Graef and Langlotz 1925–33) or in the smaller urban and countryside locations, show that the potter was called upon to provide the consumer with pots that could be dedicated to the deity, and many are of indifferent quality. Some were pieces that had already been used in the world outside the sanctuary (worn or mended), but many were certainly made specifically for dedication, as small-scale or miniature votives, and had no task to perform in everyday life (cf. Figure VI: 14, from Brauron). There was a range of wares found in sanctuaries, not all of them dedications, such as figured mixing-bowls and cups that suggest feasting and drinking, cult vessels such as peri-rrhanteria (holy water basins), and coarse wares (cf. Pemberton 1989a). The fact that the pottery has survived has given it a higher profile in the study of sanctuaries than it had in reality, as the sanctuaries were banks that regularly guarded large quantities of costly objects of silver and gold; these have been looted and melted down (Vickers and Gill 1994: 55–62). The pottery is the detritus of a much richer total.

Figure III: 13 Athenian red-figure chous, late fifth century BC.
Ht 23.6 cm.

MAN'S WORLD

It is now time to turn and look at that other world within Athens – the man's world – and see what need he had for the potter. Men inhabited the world outside the house; they dominated it, and their needs were many and various. The potter would receive requests that touched public life, religion, trades, work of all sorts, and recreation as well. It is still not clear how the marketing of pottery functioned: were there patrons who ordered pots to be made and scenes to be painted? to what extent did the state issue any orders for vases? and what of the merchants and traders who were to take the goods abroad?

What of state business? The Athenian men in their capacity as annual officers of the state would need to order, from a local potter, objects that were dictated by the state's needs. We can point to such objects as official measures (Figure III: 14; Lang and Crosby 1964; Miller 1993: 126, n. 107 (bronze examples)) – a measure of liquid in the jug (270 cc), a dry measure in the cylinder (1800 cc). On the jug there is painted, before firing, the ligature of two joined letters, a Greek *delta* and a Greek *eta*, the two initial letters of a word that is written out in full round the cylinder: *demosion*, meaning 'public property', therefore a standard measure. The dry measure also carries a seal of Athena's head which was impressed in the clay when it was still wet – presumably another mark of official endorsement. A number of these have survived, and the DE ligature is also to be found on some black cups (Figure III: 14, centre) that were used for the drinking that officials of state, then as now, were dutifully forced to endure (Rotroff and Oakley 1992: 36–7). There were also official water-clocks for the law courts (Figure III: 14, above), by which the speeches of the public and

Figure III: 14 Athenian public pots: water-clock, liquid and dry measures, and black cup, from the Athenian Agora, fifth and fourth centuries BC. Ht of water-clock 17.2 cm.

private orators and politicians were timed (Thompson and Wycherley 1972: 55; Ober and Hedrick 1993: 87–9; Camp 1994: no. 123a). The device was very simple, consisting of two bowls that had a hole that could be stoppered when required. The one found has the name of the political division whose property it was: 'of Antiochis'; and the capacity is indicated by two signs showing the Greek letter *chi*, an abbreviation for two choes which would have been the equivalent of about six litres and which emptied in about six minutes.

One might also consider here the small thimble-sized pots used for drugs and medicine – thirteen were found in the annexe of the state prison, not far from the city centre of Athens, and were most likely the containers for the executioner's hemlock (Lang 1978; Vanderpool 1980; Ober and Hedrick 1993: figure 20). It will be recalled that Plato, when writing an account of the death of Socrates in the *Phaedo* (117a–c), was careful to note that Socrates was not allowed to use any of the deadly hemlock for an offering: the executioner told him that they prepared just the requisite dose. Socrates had asked 'What do you say about pouring a libation to some deity from this draught? May I or may I not?' 'Socrates,' said the jailer, 'we grind only as much as we think is sufficient.' The official dose was carefully adjusted.

Some potters were also given the state commission to produce hundreds of black-figure oil-containers that were prizes in the Panathenaic Games every four years: Athena on one side (e.g. Figure II: 16), the specific race on the other (e.g. Figure V: 4). Over fourteen hundred were needed on each of these four-yearly occasions, a lucrative order for any potter to receive (Johnston 1987; Neils 1992: 29–51; Hamilton 1992: 127–34). Winners of the four-horse race, the most prestigious victory, received no fewer than 140 amphorae full of oil. It was the contents that were much more valuable than the containers, though personal and family pride will have played a part where Panathenaic prize amphorae have been found in tombs of athletes (for the markets for the amphorae, see Neils 1992: 48–50). Given the possible size of the commission, it should be noted that few potters or painters actually put their names on the vases to advertise their business. They cannot have been prohibited from doing so, as a few of them did indeed add their names (Frel 1973; Neils 1992: 41; Williams 1995: 143, 156).

To move from the official to the personal level, the young men who trained in the palaestrae and gymnasia for the Panathenaic and other games would need their own oil flask for cleaning and sweetening themselves after the training session or after the actual race. Again the potter provided the necessary item in the shape of the aryballos, a small sphere with narrow neck and broad lip on which to run the oil (Beazley 1931; Haspels 1931). This was hung on the wrist and fitted the hand very comfortably. When the athlete was exercising or washing, the flask would be hung, maybe with the scraper, sponge and clothes on a nearby tree for later use.

The work ethic is of course a recent phenomenon and was not to the fore in antiquity. If a man was unlucky enough to have to work in the service of another man to earn his living, then in the many lines of business there would be need to call on the potter. For instance, the shoemaker would require a basin in which to soften his leather for his made-to-measure method of shoe-making – and the potter could provide him with the popular all-purpose bowl we have seen before (Ziomecki 1975: 34–5). Another example takes us out into the countryside and to the vineyards (Figure III: 15), where at the time of the grape harvest the basins for collecting the juice and the various types of cups, jugs and containers – all

Figure III: 15 Athenian red-figure column-krater, from Spina, *c.* 460 BC. Ht 43 cm.

made of clay – were much in demand (Sparkes 1976; cf. Immerwahr 1992). The large containers for casking the wine (Figure III: 16) were the transport jars (amphorae) which were produced in their thousands and have been found all over the Mediterranean world and beyond, marking various trade routes (Grace 1961; Koehler 1979; Empereur and Garlan 1986; cf. Peacock and Williams 1986). The jars were also used for the transport of corn, oil, fish sauce, etc., and were one of the shapes most in demand from the potters. The shape made them extremely functional: the narrow mouth could be stoppered with wax or clay; the two vertical handles enabled the jar to be lifted when full; the narrow base provided an extra handle when the contents were being poured out, and the narrowing to the base also enabled the jars to be stacked neatly together in a ship's hold; and they could be fixed in the ground to keep the contents cool.

We are today so accustomed to a variety of different materials used to make containers (glass, plastic, metal, etc.) that it is interesting to be reminded how many were made of clay in antiquity. This is true also of beehives. Hives were made of terracotta and had special lids which were tied to the body of the hive and had a small semicircle cut away for the entrance (Graham 1975; Crane 1983: 45–51; Crane and Graham 1985; Osborne 1994: no. 93). The inside was left rough for the building up of the comb. The whole contraption was stacked horizontally with others, to form a wall of hives. Examples of walls of hives are still to be seen in present-day Greece.

There remains the area of men's life in recreation. One of the most important occasions in the life of the man with time to spare was the drinking party, the symposion (Murray 1990a; Schmitt Pantel 1992). We are shown the elements of the party in the images that decorated the painted vases (e.g. Figure III: 17). In fashioning their drinking cups the potters produced some of their finest creations – elegant shapes with high-quality drawing; the best known products of the potters' skill. On these occasions wine flowed, music sounded, voices were lifted in song and conversation, lamps were lit, games were played and cups raised to the lips (Vickers 1978). Girls, hired for the evening, danced and played musical instruments, and then joined the men on the couches for more play. Wine was decanted from the storage jars into the mixing bowls, and then the slave boys rushed to and fro, dipping their jugs into the bowls that contained the mixture of wine and water, to fill the stemmed cups and mugs that the guests held up for their attention (Vierneisel and Kaeser 1990).

The images that decorated the different shapes of drinking cup (see Chapter V) were there to instruct, to amuse, to stimulate and to titillate, and they sometimes show the effects the wine might have – it could make you extrovert, merry, vocal, amorous, or legless. On the vases the painters often presented not-so-solemn statements about the effects of overindulgence.

Figure III: 16 Rhodian, Cnidian, Chian and Roman transport
amphorae, from the Athenian Agora, pre-86 BC.

When inside you, drink has only two ways it can go: up or down. The potter
once again had to be prepared to supply a shape for either eventuality, and
the painters present images to show what solution the potters provided for
dealing with both problems. He might furnish the symposiasts with a bowl
by the couch, in fact once again the popular all-purpose bowl, with its
distinguishing stripe (Figure III: 11), capacious enough for the most
wayward regurgitator. A slave boy would be on hand to hold the drinker's
head and keep his beard well out of the line of fire. Or the drinker might
use a jug so fashioned that it was capacious enough for the most unsteady
and casual urinator. The type of plain jug used is a common one, with
high-swung handle for ease of use and access (Sparkes and Talcott 1970:
64–5). An older man might take the wise precaution of seeking assistance
from a slave boy, so that his conversation or his drunken singing should
not be interrupted by minor inconveniences (Figure III: 18). The stick the
boy is holding here no doubt also belongs to the older man; it is in safer

Figure III: 17 Athenian red-figure cup, *c.* 480 BC. Diam. 31.5 cm.

keeping with the slave boy than with his preoccupied master. He also carries the knapsack of goodies, maybe for the next party to which they are making their way. As Knauer comments:

> The reveler's grand gesture, half-open mouth, and inspired upward gaze seem to reflect his devotion to the god whose gift he must have sampled to a great extent, as well as to express his pathetic urgency. Yet, because of his aroused state, nature's call is forced to wait. The boy's attitude, however, is calm and matter of fact. While shouldering his master's knotty stick, together with the strings of a picnic basket, neatly covered by a fringed embroidered napkin, he proffers the large jug and steadies it to wait things out.
>
> (1986: 94–5)

Potters then had to be men for all seasons, for all occasions. It is a mistake to think of Greek pottery and its images solely as expressions of the potter's and painter's imaginative vision or to get too carried away into the realms of aesthetics and connoisseurship, with its accent on the figured pieces. There is also the more basic aspect of the craftsman's skill – that of meeting all the practical demands that society made of him.

Figure III: 18   Athenian red-figure chous, *c.* 460 BC. Ht 23.4 cm.

BACKGROUND READING

For the making of pottery, see Richter 1923; Hampe and Winter 1962 and 1965; Peacock 1982; Sparkes 1991a, chapter II; Hemelrijk 1991.

For the treatment of shapes in general, see the background reading for Chapter I and Richter and Milne 1935; Boardman 1974, chapter 9 and 1975a, chapter 5; Kanowski 1984; Boardman 1989a, chapter 9; Sparkes 1991a, chapter IV.

Most of the study of Greek pottery has been devoted to the fine and figured shapes; for the coarser shapes, see Sparkes and Talcott 1970. For transport amphorae, see Grace 1961; Koehler 1979; Empereur and Garlan 1986; Peacock and Williams 1986; Whitbread 1995.

For Athenian subjects, see Webster 1972; on death: Kurtz and Boardman 1971; Garland 1985; I. Morris 1992; on women: Cameron and Kuhrt 1983/1993; Fantham *et al*. 1994; Blundell 1995; on weddings: Oakley and Sinos 1993; on private life: Jenkins 1986; on sanctuaries: Bremmer 1994: chapter III; on public life: Lang 1960; Ober and Hedrick 1993; on symposia: Lissarrague 1990a; Murray 1990a; Vierneisel and Kaeser 1990; Schmitt Pantel 1992.

CHAPTER IV

'A VERY CURIOUS
PHENOMENON'

——— •◆• ———

The quotation that forms the heading for this chapter is taken from an article by Martin Robertson. 'Greek painted vases,' he wrote, 'looked at with detachment, are a very curious phenomenon' (Robertson 1951: 151). After a while students of Greek pottery maybe find it difficult to look at them 'with detachment'; certainly it is difficult, once you are used to them, to distance yourself from them and appreciate how curious they really are.

Perhaps their most curious aspect is their combination of the craft of the potter and the skill and imagination of the draughtsman. To be sure, there have been other cultures before and after the Hellenic in which pictures are to be found on pottery. One need only step back into the Late Bronze Age in Greece itself to encounter figured decoration on pottery or move forward into the European tradition and look at late fifteenth-century Majolica or Sèvres porcelain of the later eighteenth century. One can of course go outside Europe for other examples. But in Greek painted pottery the conjunction of the potter's shapes and painted scenes is more basic: the pieces are less elaborately decorated than in the later European tradition; they were popular products, not for the élite; and they were issued in thousands over many centuries. More than that, the subjects that decorate the various shapes are not transferred or repeated designs as in willow pattern (on replicas, see Oakley 1992: 200–3). Also, in some centres of production, notably Athens, there is a whole range of subjects from manly pursuits such as horse-riding and hunting, sport of a more amorous kind, religious ritual such as moving in procession to a sanctuary or making an offering at an altar, humble crafts such as shoemaking and carpentry, and the sad occasion of the laying out of the dead. So the serious and light-hearted aspects of human life are there, along with the heroic, the fantastic and the divine. On occasion the grandeur and intensity of feeling evoked surpass anything that Meissen or Sèvres accomplished or even contemplated.

So it is not surprising that scholars and laymen alike have been attracted to the images. In the nineteenth century and earlier it was mainly the subject matter that claimed attention, whether legendary scenes or vignettes from everyday life (see Chapter II), and subject matter will be the topic of the next chapter. But over the last hundred years it has been connoisseurship – study of the individual style of the painting and the hands of the painters – that has been the main thrust of the study. That thrust looks as though it may be losing momentum, may be less vigorous now; it is certainly being questioned as a valid approach, is losing its credibility in some quarters, and is becoming a smaller proportion of the whole study. Here is a recent extravagant parallel that has been made:

> Connoisseurship today enjoys a reputation not unlike that of Proust's Princesse de Luxembourg at Balbec: recognized by some as the *grande dame* of art history, viewed by others as an expensive and aging tart.
>
> (Maginnis 1990: 104)

So let us now consider style and connoisseurship – its foundations and its methods, its triumphs and its perceived drawbacks and limitations.

THE METHOD AND ITS APPLICATION TO GREEK VASES

Giovanni Morelli (1816–91) always was, and continues to be, a controversial figure (Wind 1963: 35–51; Wollheim 1974: 177–201; Kurtz 1985b: 240–1; Maginnis 1990). He trained as a doctor in the University of Munich in the middle years of the nineteenth century, and brought the methods of clinical observation, in which he was schooled, to the study of Renaissance painting. In the words of a critic invented by Morelli himself, his method 'savoured more of an anatomist ... than of a student of art' (Morelli 1892–3: 35). What he looked for was consistency within the work of one artist and a distinctiveness that marked off that artist's work from the work of others. As a start he tended to look for characteristic renderings that were signatures of the artist – ears, hands, drapery, folds, musculature. Today (see e.g. Wind 1963: plate 8; Wollheim 1974: 182, figure 1 and 191, figure 5; Morris 1993: 42, figure 1) the surgeon's severed ears and hands look distinctly odd, not to say crude, renderings of the originals – he was an anatomist indeed! Many since Morelli have spoken of the artist giving himself away and have used comparisons on those lines, for example 'as a criminal might be spotted by a fingerprint' (Wind 1963: 41). Such a method as Morelli's tends to be frowned upon in these less certain days (Elsner 1990; Maginnis 1990): surely formulae can be imitated by pupils and others, and surely the artist himself may vary formulae with age, change of eyesight, or some such cause? But Morelli's *Critical Studies* of the 1890s (Morelli 1892–3) was a necessary revolution for its time, and if modern techniques of attribution are more sophisticated than they were a hundred years ago, if the eye has been displaced, or at least buttressed, by the lens of science, be it camera, microscope or ray gun, and if 'the structure of the eye and its functioning' are more clearly understood (Maginnis 1990: 108), nonetheless it was the need to look closely at paintings, to sort out detail, to banish or at least reduce the element of intuition, to depend on the lines drawn or the brush strokes executed by the draughtsman and play down the emphasis on general effect – it was these approaches that proved a proper road to travel. As we have been reminded (Wollheim 1974: 178, quoting Morelli 1892–3: 74 n.), Morelli was taught as a student of medicine that observation and comparison were indispensable to the naturalist, and he himself added '(and to the art-connoisseur)'.

Morelli's most famous follower was Bernard Berenson (1865–1956) (Brown 1979; Kurtz 1985b: 241–3; Maginnis 1990). And, although he is considered to have had a deeper sensitivity than Morelli, he was perhaps more suspect, because of the lure the art market had for him and because of his work as purchasing agent for such collectors as Mrs Gardner and Lord Duveen. He also worked in his later years from photographs – not the most accurate method of attribution for canvas paintings.

Before the end of the nineteenth century German scholars had already adopted an approach to attribution in the study of Greek vase-painting that anticipated Morelli's methods. There was by that time certainly enough Greek material to work on: we noted earlier the thousands of vases found at Vulci (see Chapter II), and the numbers were growing all the time. Also the standard of publications was much higher than before, for example Theodor Lau, Heinrich Brunn and P.F. Krell's *Die griechischen Vasen* of vases in Munich (Lau 1877), and Genick and Furtwängler's *Griechische Keramik* of the Berlin material (Genick and Furtwängler 1883). I also mentioned in this connection (Chapter II) that photography was beginning to be used more widely as the century drew to its close. But there were difficulties: many vases were fragmentary; many vases were dispersed to different museums both in Europe and in America; even fragments from the same vase might be thousands of miles apart; many were 'restored' with a covering of thick black paint and a complete but invented picture substituted for the real but lacunose one beneath. Nor were all vases easily available for study: either they were in private collections or, if in public hands, they were felt to be the private property of the museum directors who had an attitude of *ius primae noctis* or *droit de seigneur* about their study. It has recently been remarked in caustic fashion that this is a principle that is still honoured in some museums today, where serious scholars are prevented from making drawings or even close examination of the material on display!

As for the vases themselves, little external help is available: there is no documentation, no Vasari, no biographies, no deeds of sale, etc., to make them 'authenticated works'. There are also very few 'signatures', but the existence of those very few led to the treatment of vases as *Meisterwerke*. The distinction between a name followed by 'epoiesen' ('made') and one followed by 'egrapsen' ('drew' or 'painted') was not always heeded; it was Furtwängler who, in one scholar's words, 'sorted it out' (von Bothmer 1987: 198).

But it was Morelli's method that reduced the importance of an investigation via the *œuvre d'art signé* and enabled study to move away from signatures. Adolf Furtwängler and other German scholars (such as Paul Hartwig and Wilhelm Klein) of the late nineteenth and early twentieth centuries made great headway, but it was the English scholar, J.D. Beazley (1885–1970), who, beginning in the first decade of this century, took the study further than any other scholar. He was knighted in 1949 and created a Companion of Honour in 1959. His connoisseurship was always of the highest quality, and it is not surprising that he attracted followers who have carried on and extended his work. His study of vase-painting concerned not only style but interpretation and iconography, techniques and chronology, etc. He was also one of the greatest all-round classical scholars of this century. He made sense of an amorphous mass of material, mainly Athenian black-figure and red-figure, and made close scrutiny of the painting – of any preliminary sketch lines (relief lines also), the surrounding decoration, the shape, all aspects of the painted object – an absolute necessity, even of the meanest work. To suggest that his method hinged only on the observation of trivial details misunderstands his whole approach. Even if he made no mention of Morelli or Berenson (Kurtz 1985b: 243), he applied similar methods to Greek vase-painting with an acumen that has not been equalled. He has been a pivotal figure in the discipline and only recently has he become a 'somewhat controversial figure' (Vickers 1987: 100). Even if the approach he adopted is now being questioned, there is no doubting the man's remarkable achievement (for sympathetic accounts, see Ashmole 1970/1985; Robertson 1976 and 1985; Isler-Kerenyi 1980; Kurtz 1985b). A recent critic pays graceful homage to him:

> The extent of his monumental achievement can only be grasped when we recall how little was known before he turned his relentless eye upon details *apparently* [my italics] trivial. Before him there was no systematic method for classifying Greek vases. By the time of his death, Beazley had made it possible to attribute the great majority of surviving pots (more or less satisfactorily, but always with only minor adjustments necessary), to over a thousand artists or groups.
>
> (Elsner 1990: 950)

Almost singlehandedly (though Beazley himself would never admit it and was always scrupulous to acknowledge the work of his predecessors and colleagues in the field), Beazley laid out a whole history of vase-painting in Athens from 600 to 300 BC (see Chapter I), from the beginnings of true black-figure down the centuries to the closing years of the red-figure technique – a complex structure showing the rise and fall of careers, the interplay between painters, the influence of one on another, the choice of themes, the effect of historical events and incidents, etc. Over a thousand painters and groups were distinguished by Beazley and others (about 400 of black-figure and 800 of red-figure) and over thirty thousand vases attributed (10,000 black-figure and 20,000 red-figure) (for the listings, see Beazley 1956; 1963; 1971; and Carpenter 1989). There is still a substantial residue of unattributed pieces and of course the number of vases is still rising, whether from controlled excavations in any of the lands that Greek artefacts reached, or from the clandestine work of the *tombaroli* amongst the tombs of cemeteries in Tuscany and elsewhere that continue to have their contents torn from their context. But now there is no Beazley to propose an attribution or to put his *imprimatur* on an attribution suggested by another scholar. This has been seen both as a problem in itself for the future of connoisseurship (Robertson 1976; cf. 1992a: 2–6) and has gone some way to a challenging of the whole approach.

Let us look briefly at some of those painters that Beazley distinguished before drawing up a balance sheet of credits and debits, concentrating on red-figure painters.

What one might call Beazley's Big Three in red-figure are the Kleophrades Painter, the Pan Painter and the Berlin Painter, all working in the first half of the fifth century BC. Beazley in a real sense created them, as they had no names and no personae before he worked on them. He wrote some of his earliest monographs on them, and in the 1930s and later produced elegant essays that brought them vividly into focus and mapped out their development.

Figure IV: 1 Athenian red-figure fragment, from the Athenian Acropolis, *c.* 510 BC. Ht 7.4 cm.

94

Figure IV: 2 Athenian red-figure amphora, from Vulci, *c.* 500–490 BC.
Ht of amphora 56 cm.

The Kleophrades Painter takes his name from a potter Kleophrades for whom one unnamed painter worked on many occasions and decorated many shapes (for the painter, see Beazley 1933/1974; see also Boardman 1975a: 91–4; Robertson 1992a: 56–66) – hence the title of convenience, the Kleophrades Painter. It is now known (and had long been suspected) that the potter Kleophrades was the son of the black-figure potter Amasis (von Bothmer 1981b; 1985a: 230–1), but this tells us nothing of the painter. Here are two details (Figures IV: 1 and 2), one from a fragment showing a lyre-player, the other the head of Dionysos. Close attention to the form of the eye and eyebrow, the ear, the nose and nostril, the mouth, the beard, etc., brings out the style of the painter. There is also a grandeur and an exaltation about his work: his figures belong to a heroic breed, solid and strong, mainly to be found on large pots such as kraters and amphorae. The energy and force of the Kleophrades Painter are best seen in the paintings he created of the legends connected with the Trojan War, for which he had a penchant (Boardman 1976).

The Pan Painter takes his modern sobriquet not from a potter for whom he worked but from a naughty rustic scene of a grossly tumescent goat

Figure IV: 3 Athenian red-figure hydria, from Capua, *c*. 460 BC. Ht of hydria 34.5 cm.

god, Pan, in pursuit of a herdsman (for the painter, see Beazley 1931/1974; see also Boardman 1975a: 180–1, 193; Robertson 1992a: 143–7). This is not a painter of grandeur and seriousness but one of delicate vivacity and humour. The reverse of the mixing bowl shows death as a mannered tableau – the hunter, Actaeon, being attacked by his own dogs on the instruction of the goddess Artemis, the falling figure arrested in mid-fall, whilst Artemis gracefully points her toe and an arrow at her victim. The Pan Painter's lines and compositions are a mixture of archaic stiffness and more supple movement. He is not interested in battles and athletic sports, and his treatment of the popular themes that do take his fancy is original and witty. Even the frightening story of Perseus and the decapitated Gorgon Medusa (Figure IV: 3) is made into a dainty ballet dance, with a surprisingly feminine Athena lifting her flimsy skirt to assist her get-away with Perseus, not escorting him out of danger but following his lead. Here is a painter with a sharp sense of the ridiculous – witness the fingertips of the headless Gorgon as she sinks operatically down. The personality of the painter – indeed of any of these painters – is built up by close observation of his line, his finish, his composition, his choice and treatment of subject, his adaptation of each picture to the shape.

Figure IV: 4 Athenian red-figure amphora, from Nola, *c.* 490 BC. Ht of amphora 41.5 cm.

The name piece of the Berlin Painter, to whom now over three hundred vases have been attributed, is an amphora in the Berlin Museum (for the painter, see Beazley 1930/1974; 1964/1989: 66–77; see also Boardman 1975a: 94–5, 111; Kurtz and Beazley 1983; Robertson 1992a: 66–83). This painter likes to spotlight subjects on the black background. His line is fluid and lively, and on occasion the single figure is divorced from all pattern (Figure IV: 4, singing an exalted song with the singer accompanying himself on the professional performer's *kithara*). Beazley showed that his propensity to paint 'mantle' figures (i.e. groups of fully clothed figures in conversation) on the less important side of his pots not only assisted in attributing paintings to this painter and in charting the rise and fall of his career (Beazley 1922), but also could be used in a parallel application to other painters adopting similar arrangements of 'mantle' figures.

Figure IV: 5   Athenian red-figure amphora, from Vulci, *c.* 450 BC.
Ht 62 cm.

Such painters and the many others worked in potteries alongside the
potters and their painter colleagues (Scheibler 1983; Sparkes 1991a). They
learned their craft from the older men and passed it on to the apprentices;
they had 'masters' and 'pupils', however one envisages the organisation.
Beazley built up a nexus of associations with words such as 'companion',
'brother', etc., a grid which is not easy to comprehend but which in a total
view speaks of a living and lively tradition of craftsmanship (Robertson
1989). To take a simple example, the Berlin Painter's stylistic approach is
continued by the painter now called the Achilles Painter (Boardman 1989a:
61, 129, 132; Oakley 1990: 58–63) in the middle years of the century. Figure
IV: 5 is his name piece: an amphora with the single, unframed picture of
the hero. One can also see the effect of the Berlin Painter in the other
technique of which the Achilles Painter was a master – white ground. Figure
I: 12 shows an Athenian soldier to compare with Achilles. He is bidding

Figure IV: 6 Athenian red-figure volute-krater, from Cervetri,
c. 490 BC. Ht of vase 63.5 cm.

Figure IV: 7 Athenian red-figure volute-krater, *c.* 490 BC. Ht 61 cm.

farewell to his wife as he goes off to war, but as this is a white-ground lekythos which was placed in a tomb, we know that the man is already dead, and the farewell is final. We can take the apprenticeship one stage further – in the next generation a painter we call the Phiale Painter (Boardman 1989a: 61–2, 132; Oakley 1990) had learned his craft from the Achilles Painter, and so the 'school', if we choose to think in those terms, continued.

The individual painters have been created not only from a close study of the way in which they draw their individual figures (whether human or animal) and of the composition of their figured scenes but also from a scrutiny of the pattern work. Let us revert to the Berlin Painter – he has always proved a useful exemplar. Most shapes boasted pattern of some kind, either framing the figured composition, if there was one, or bordering the vase: mouth, lip, handles, foot. Figure IV: 6 illustrates the upper part of a volute-krater which carries figured decoration of a duel on the neck; the body was painted black. Above the neck the heavy rim carries a complex floral pattern. A similar shape, also painted by the Berlin Painter, carries the main scene on the body – it shows Demeter sending Triptolemos away in his winged car to spread agriculture to the world (Boardman 1975a: figure 154). There are no figures on the neck of this vase, but once again a complex pattern on the rim (Figure IV: 7). The scheme of decoration on the first krater is a key pattern stopt by saltire cross (St Andrews cross) in squares above a double floral. When we transfer our attention to the second krater, we see an almost identical pattern (apart from a Greek cross in square), and in fact the double floral here is a special design found only in the work of this painter, whose style was initially isolated on the basis of the figures. It is in the accumulation of details such as these that the vases have been sorted and attributed. This method works not only for quality pieces but for the lesser lights as well. The nature of the method means that it must work with material of whatever quality, period or source, provided there are enough diagnostic elements. It has been well said that 'there is no place to get a knife in' (Robertson 1985: 27). Once the careful scrutiny of detail, whether of figure drawing or patternwork, has been carried out, such aspects as composition, choice of topic and effect of subject matter must also be considered. The movement from style to content and back again must be continuous.

Beazley concerned himself chiefly with Athenian red-figure and white-ground and also with black-figure, with the hacks as well as the quality pieces. Figure I: 6 shows the superb neck-amphora with Achilles killing Penthesileia; Exekias signed it as potter, but attention to the style of the painting showed that the painter was the same as the one who else-where signed 'Exekias painted and potted' and on other vases signed 'Exekias painted'. It was then possible to show that some unsigned vases were painted by the same hand. We have seen that Amasis the potter was the father of Kleophrades the potter. We cannot be certain that Amasis was also a painter, though many believe so (Beazley 1951/1986: 57–62/52–7; Boardman 1974: 54–6; von Bothmer 1985a: 53–8; Mertens 1987), but the painter who decorated most of the vases signed by Amasis the potter is still more safely called the Amasis Painter (cf. Figures I: 7 and III: 7). These are two of the very few names of potters and painters that we know from Athenian black-figure; the rest have been summoned into life by a study of the details of the painting, and as with the red-figure painters have been given names of convenience. Beazley also made excursions into the wilder realms of vase-paintings executed by painters in Etruria where local painters borrowed and adapted ideas that they selected from the pottery imported from Athens (Beazley 1947; see also del Chiaro 1974; Martelli 1987; Padgett *et al.* 1993: 227–67).

Humfry Payne, Beazley's favourite pupil, explored with him some areas of Athenian black-figure (Beazley and Payne 1929) and went on himself to sort out Corinthian painted pottery of the seventh and sixth centuries (Payne 1931; 1933; cf. Amyx 1988). Other followers have broadened and deepened the study of Athenian vase-painting, for example Robertson (e.g. 1992a on red-figure), von Bothmer (e.g. 1976 on Euphronios; 1985a on the Amasis Painter) and Williams (e.g. 1983a on Sophilos; 1991b on Onesimos). Other scholars have extended the method into other areas, for example the rather pedestrian Laconian (Shefton 1954; Stibbe 1972; cf. Figure I: 8) or the colourful and more lighthearted Caeretan hydriai (Hemelrijk 1984; cf. Figure V: 5). The method has been carried back in time to the Geometric (Davison 1961; Coldstream 1968) and beyond, to Mycenaean (Vermeule and Karageorghis 1982; cf. Morris 1993), whilst the potters and painters amongst the Greeks of South Italy and Sicily, who owed so much to the Athenian tradition but were able to carry it to more elaborate lengths, have been sorted out into local workshops with individual painters (Trendall 1967; 1983; 1987; 1989; Trendall and Cambitoglou 1978 and 1982; 1983).

It should not be supposed that the process of attribution is easy or to be approached lightly; a sensitive eye, a phenomenal memory and a chalcenteric ability to face thousands of vases are only three of the qualities that are needed. Figure IV: 8 poses some of the problems to be faced. More than thirty years ago a cup was attributed to the Berlin Painter for which the London volute-krater we saw earlier (Figure IV: 6) provides a close comparison (Robertson 1958) – but is it close enough? After much hesitation Beazley was disposed to accept the connection:

> Miss Talcott saw that this cup was curiously close, in many respects, to the Berlin Painter, and suggested that it might be from his hand, his earliest work. This view has been persuasively argued by Martin

Figure IV: 8 Athenian red-figure cup, from the Athenian Agora,
c. 500 BC. Diam. c. 18 cm.

Robertson ... and should, I think, be accepted. There are differences
which made me hesitate, but the resemblances are so great as to
outweigh them.

(Beazley 1963: 213–14)

However, further study has suggested that, although close, the cup belongs
somewhere on the borders of the artist, allied but not identical (Kurtz 1983).
This disassociation of the cup from the Berlin Painter is rather ironic as
the cup is signed by a potter, a man called Gorgos, and there was always
the possibility that he may have been a painter as well. Such is the instinctive
yearning for names! That nexus of associations that Beazley built up is still
able to cope with the fine tuning – indeed it must do so; the worst service
that the followers of the method can do is to assume that Beazley's work
is set in concrete. 'There is no place for a Bible in scholarship' (Robertson
1992a: 6).

BALANCE SHEET

If accepted, the method can be applied in any circumstances, but there are
dangers and pitfalls, not to mention the *petitio principii* of the whole system.
As Robertson has well put it (1976: 36), 'some people ... accept Beazley's
attributions as a matter of faith, others ... dismiss the whole thing as something of a confidence trick; both, surely, mistaken attitudes'. Let us first
assume, as we have already done, that the method is viable, and look at
what has been gained by such an approach. Then we shall consider the

question mark that hangs over the approach and see what the arguments against the method are. Major objections are being made: that it is flawed, if not completely fraudulent; that it creates a false picture of working conditions and associations; that it raises the status of potters and vase-painters beyond what is credible; that it diverts interest from other avenues of approach.

NAMES OF CRAFTSMEN

But first, we turn our attention to the named craftsmen. Those vases which carry a proper name and either or both of the words 'epoiesen' ('made') and 'egrapsen' ('painted') were naturally ones that attracted attention in the early days of the study of Greek vases (cf. Chapter II). They have in some ways laid a false trail with their emphasis on what has been called 'the artist as hero' and the importance of the *œuvre d'art signé*. Their significance has been debated recently, and their meaning called into question.

We have seen how it is only a very minute proportion of the total output of figured vases that has survived, and out of the small percentage there is another trivial number of 'signed' pieces. Of these, Athenian vases carry the greatest share (see e.g. Sophilos, Figure I: 5; Nearchos, Figure VI: 13; Phrynos, Figure V: 1; Exekias, Figures I: 6, II: 17; Taleides, Figure II: 15; Andokides, Figure I: 10; Oikopheles, Figure IV: 12; Smikros, Figure IV: 13; Euphronios, Figure II: 1; Gorgos, Figure IV: 8; Meidias, Figure II: 13) with the remainder divided between Corinthian, Boeotian (Kilinski 1992), South Italian (As(s)teas, Figures I: 18, V: 3) and a few others (Sparkes 1991a: 66–8, 113–16). What prompted the addition of the names? It can hardly be self-advertisement or pride, though some names occur more frequently than others. The addition of names seems to be more fashionable in some generations than in others (Williams 1995), but the numbers are statistically meaningless.

The help that such names can give resides in the grouping of individual workmanship, the origins of the craftsmen (e.g. Thracian, Syrian, Lydian), the occasional addition of a father's name, and the tentative conclusions that can be drawn about the organisation of the pottery shops. As for the drawbacks, these are perceived as a narrowing of attention to the producers of the pottery; an emphasis on the individual 'artist' rather than on the wider view of the craft; the assumption that the words 'epoiesen' and 'egrapsen' refer to the actual making and painting of the vases by individuals, when they may have a more general application to the workshop; and the possibility that the procedure and the names are transferred from metalworking (for a discussion of these suggestions, see recently Robertson 1992a: 2–3; 1992b: 132–3).

CREDIT

Direct observation and the evidence of contexts show that vase-painting, as other crafts, developed from generation to generation. What Beazley and others did was to refine that development from the general to the particular. One of the most important legacies that has been passed on is the requirement that emphasis should be placed on the meticulous investigation of all aspects of the painting. This may seem basic but is not always followed, even now. This is especially necessary when dealing with fragments, as fragments have edges that may hide the tip of a finger, the edge of a garment, the frill of a snake. Also, with the older excavations, fragments could be scattered over more than one museum, and on occasion close scrutiny is continuing to reunite the scattered fragments. A prime example is the cup attributed to the late sixth-century red-figure painter Oltos which is now composed of fragments that are scattered over two continents, three countries and six museums: Rome (Villa Giulia), Florence, Heidelberg, Brunswick, Baltimore and Bowdoin (Maine) (Beazley 1933: plate X). As Morelli said, 'the only true record for the connoisseur is the work of art itself' (Morelli 1892–3: 26–7).

On the basis of stylistic analysis, the fixing of craftsmen in a particular generation enables their output to be set beside other work of the time (sculpture, literature, etc.) to build up or reflect the ethos of a generation. The Kleophon Painter and others, working in Athens in the Periklean period (Boardman 1989a: chapter 3), mirror the same feeling that is expressed in the Parthenon – serious, high-minded idealism in the service of the state (Figure I: 13); it looks indeed as though the Kleophon Painter had borrowed ideas from the Parthenon frieze itself, as he and others may well have done. The rich style of the following wartime generation (e.g. Figures II: 13 and V: 9) peopled with its band of yearning, love-sick, languid females, decked out in clinging draperies (Burn 1987), can be paralleled with contemporary sculpture such as the figures from the Nike balustrade on the Athenian Acropolis (Boardman 1985: figures 129–30).

The sorting out of specific craftsmen has created instances of individual talent with preferences in compositions, subjects and shapes, as we have seen. It has also been possible to trace the stylistic development of a painter. The painter Onesimos is a case in point (for the painter, see Ohly-Dumm 1981; Sparkes 1985; Williams 1991b). In his early years he painted grand, vital, rollicking satyrs, bursting the frame of the tondo (Figure IV: 9). A decade later in his career (on present estimate) his figures shrank to more reserved proportions (Figure IV: 10); they retreated, as it were, from the border of the design. In this contrast here I am reminded of Robert Graves's poem 'Ogres and Pygmies'. Of the ogres he said:

They had long beards and stinking arm-pits,
They were wide mouthed, long yarded and great bellied.

Figure IV: 9 Athenian red-figure cup, from Orvieto, *c.* 500 BC. Diam. 24.8 cm.

Whereas the pygmies were:

> the sweet-cupid-lipped and tassel-yarded
> Delicate-stomached dwellers
> in Pygmy Alley.

The individual style of Onesimos can be followed through the changes, stage by stage, from ogre to pygmy.

The individual craftsmen working with potters and other painters shared their ideas, and thus associations and maybe rivalries were built up – at the next bench, across the street, in another part of the town and still further away (Thompson 1984). The grid has been extended, as we saw, down the generations, sometimes from father to son and beyond. We know from

Figure IV: 10 Athenian red-figure cup, *c.* 490 BC. Diam. of picture 12.2 cm.

signatures, rare though they are, that the techniques of potting and painting were handed down in families. Such a framework of contemporary and continuing associations frees the whole tradition from the rigid division into invented compartments that obtains in other, prehistoric cultures, and it breathes life into the workings of the industry.

We know a good deal about Athenian history and Athenian art in the fifth and fourth centuries. When we move to other areas and other times, for example South Italy and Sicily (as potters and painters themselves did from Athens towards the end of the fifth century, see Chapter I), the historical record becomes sparse, and the development of painted pottery (in particular and in general) takes on a major role in helping to understand the dark areas of its history and relations between Greek and native inhabitants. Also, with the growth of local industries and the reduction of imported pottery from Athens, some of the local effects of the break between Athens and the West, occasioned by the Athenian invasion of Sicily in 415 BC, can be judged through the observation of the distinctive work and the interrelationships of individual craftsmen.

Much was once made of the help vase-paintings could provide for missing panel-paintings, less so now but still important (Barron 1972). Some vase-painters were more influenced than others; some give the impression of being more accurate in conveying the effect of panel pictures. The white-ground cups and lekythoi with their use of varied colours against a light background have been felt, and rightly, to bring us nearer to the panel pictures and compositions that we read of in the texts (Pollitt 1990: chapter 8; Scheibler 1994). Their effect can also be seen on red-figure with the multi-level arrangement so inimical to shapes that veer away from the line of vision.

Because the initial study of vase-painting began in the context of art-history, there has been a tendency to link attribution to quality or at least to 'artistic self-consciousness'. Experiments with modern anonymous pot-painters have demonstrated that 'individuals are always somewhat different from one another in their motor habits or motor performances' (Hill 1977: 2). That is, subconscious idiosyncracies are personal to us all, and the qual-itative elements need to be separated from the mechanical; it is the latter that defy imitation.

> *All* hand-made products have individual variation. . . . Moreover, such products can be ascribed to their individual (unnamed) makers, so long as three conditions are met: 1) there must be numerous examples of precisely the same product . . .; 2) the product must exhibit sufficient complexity to make it possible to measure the individual variation . . .; and 3) the product must have been made by more than a single individual (but significantly *fewer* individuals than there are examples of the product).
>
> (Hill in Morris 1993: 57)

On such a theory the paucity of names should not be a drawback, and Athenian painted pottery at least would seem to comply with all three conditions.

DEBIT

What then of the debit side to the practice of connoisseurship on Greek painted pottery? Is anything really to be gained from knowing that two vases were painted by the same man and of inventing a name for him when one does not exist?

Beazley died in 1970, and inevitably a reaction to his work and his tradition and to what has been seen as his pernicious influence has grown up (e.g. Hoffmann 1979; 1985–6). How much has been sacrificed to this emphasis on attribution? Over ten years ago, a French scholar remarked that 'concern over attribution has for many decades sterilised the study of

Attic pottery' (Bruneau 1975: 451), and more recently it has been claimed (with some justification) that 'the tyranny of the artist over the study of Greek painted pottery has been close to absolute' (Osborne 1991: 255). Indeed, is the most important fact, if fact it is, about a fourth-century Athenian red-figure lebes gamikos (Arias, Hirmer and Shefton 1962: plates 225–8; Simon and Hirmer 1976/1981: plates 236–7; Boardman 1989a: figure 388) and an Athenian pelike of the same period (Figure IV: 11) that they were both painted by the same man, the so-called Marsyas Painter (Boardman 1989a: 190–2)? The wedding bowl has the scene of a wedding, but it was found in a tomb in the Crimea. The pelike was found in a tomb in the cemetery of the town of Kameiros on the island of Rhodes. How and why did they reach their separate destinations? And what of the story of Peleus and Thetis that the pelike carries – a mythical wedding scene, if rather an unconventional one, as the sea-nymph Thetis kept changing her shape to escape the unwanted attentions of her pursuer? Does not the story have funerary significance? And is not study of that significance of more importance than the identity of the painter?

The very viability of Morelli's method and of Beazley's similar approach has been challenged. In an uncertain age we are less sure that the signs have validity; we are less ready to believe in straight and final answers – this is his, but this is not his. What is style anyway? Is it the man? Sherlock Holmes and Freud have been ranged beside Morelli as purveyors of creeds that are now outworn: clues and symptoms do not always signify (Elsner 1990).

Recently an exhibition on Rembrandt was on view at the National Gallery in London (Bomford *et al.* 1988). Here is an artist who has come under the closest scrutiny in recent years, and all manner of techniques are being used to weed out the non-Rembrandts from the true canon: X-rays, cross-sections, neutron activation autoradiography, energy-dispersive X-ray micro-analysis – in fact it was said at the time of the exhibition that 'the paintings somehow become laboratory specimens, like corpses laid out for inspection next to the pathologist's report' (Vaizey 1988). We seem to be back with Dr Morelli!

In the matter of Greek vases, it is claimed that without 'essential documentary sources', without letters, contracts, deeds of sale, etc., there is much we are expected to take on trust. We leap out of the plane with the flimsiest of parachutes. We have no names for the majority of the artists, few signatures *in toto*, far fewer than 1 per cent (Oakley 1992: 198–200). So most painters are imaginary constructs given crazy names: Elbows Out, the Worst Painter, Fat Boys, the Painter of the Woolly Satyrs. These oddly named craftsmen, it is said, are not real people; they are not, and do not have, personalities; they are inventions, flat cardboard cutouts (turn them sideways and they disappear); they have no social or historical reality. We have only their work by which we can know them, raised into sight by the eye of the connoisseur alone; they are not 'real men'.

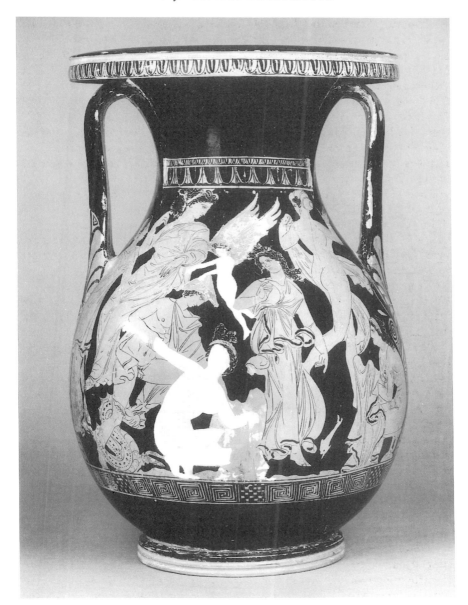

Figure IV: 11 Athenian red-figure pelike, from Kameiros (Rhodes), *c.* 360–350 BC. Ht 43.3 cm.

And who is to set the parameters of talent? Beazley wondered whether the Kleophrades Painter might also on stylistic grounds have painted in his later years a shoddy series of booted trollops (Beazley 1928: 27; 1947/1989: 235/34; Caskey and Beazley 1963: 54). The comparison may make one shudder – why should it? Talent can decay and die; if the method leads to this conclusion, then you can't just simply jettison the method because you don't like the result. But the question arises: how many other examples of deplorable hackwork might actually be lurking in the unrecognised output of a finer painter at the close of his career? One can never know the whole output of a craftsman; it is possible that some of Beazley's discrete painters may soon be seen as one.

Even if we accept the attributions, where do they lead? Is this not mere classification, taxonomy – dates, executants and the moment of production? It has been said that it is 'hard to go from formal analysis to the use of the vases as documents of their time and space' (Pinney 1984b: 420). And what is all this talk of 'masters' and 'pupils' and 'schools', etc.? Do we not presume to know too much and invent too much about the organisation of the craft? The presence of sculptural dedications and inscriptions on the Athenian Acropolis that may show pots and potters or include the word 'kerameus' (Beazley 1944/1989: 103–7/48–9) has usually been interpreted to show that the potters were men of substance. More recently the notion has been challenged and the word 'kerameus' connected with the *deme* 'Kerameis' which would accommodate many other categories of citizen besides potters (Vickers and Gill 1994: 93–5). Only one potter, Oikopheles, actually owns up to being a 'kerameus' (Figure IV: 12).

What of the allied notion that the potters and painters mixed with the great and the good, as has been claimed? On Figure IV: 13 the painter Smikros who 'signed' this vase has written his own name beside a young man absorbed in the music of the pipe-girl Helike at an aristocratic symposion (Beazley 1944/1989: 101/47). Was he not indulging in mere wish-fulfilment (cf. Vermeule 1965)? Any job in a pottery was menial, the conditions intolerable, the status low, the products cheap and myriad. It has been pointed out that the ethnographic record of traditional potters shows that they counted themselves a success when they were able to give up being a potter, and that 'an acknowledged master potter may have standing amongst fellow potters, may even command higher prices, and still be only a potter as far as the larger society is concerned' (Vitelli 1992: 552). Skill should not be assumed to confer high status.

And do not the names of the potters and painters that we do know such as Brygos and Syriskos, Lydos and Skythes suggest that they at least were foreigners and slaves; the names mean 'Phrygian', 'Little Syrian', 'Lydian' and 'Skythian'. Others such as Onesimos and Epiktetos have names which are nicknames, meaning 'Profitable' and 'Acquired'; others are called 'Little' and 'Large' (Smikros and Makron; the former is the one who imagined

Figure IV: 12 Athenian black-figure dish, from Peristeri (Attica), fifth century BC. Diam. 12 cm.

himself lying on a couch at the symposion, Figure IV: 13). The nicknames might again point to slave status. Also, have we not been seduced by false comparisons with Renaissance artists and their schools, by the status of eighteenth-century porcelain makers, by the hype perpetrated by d'Hancarville for Sir William Hamilton (see Chapter II), by nineteenth-century ideas about the dignity of labour and the Arts and Crafts movement (Vickers and Gill 1994: 82–3), by the very existence now of 'art-potters' such as Bernard Leach and Lucie Rie? And what of those vases which do not lend themselves to this method of study? Are they not to be studied at all? Moreover has not the very survival of thousands of vases

Figure IV: 13 Athenian red-figure stamnos, *c.* 520 BC. Ht of
vase 38.5 cm.

given them an unwarranted importance – 'that great curse'? Finally, are we
not led too much by the art market with its insistence on personal names,
attributed works and high prices – that art market that encourages the clandestine tearing of pots from their contexts?

The attack on the Beazley school has been strong, not to say savage. It
would be sad and counterproductive if it created a reactionary response
among the partisans of connoisseurship: dig in the defences, put up the
barricades, repel the opposition. I also think it would be sad and equally
counterproductive if connoisseurship were abandoned. As in most polemic,
there is truth on both sides and a balance must be sought. It is time to
play down the search for attributions but not to jettison it altogether; not
to be seduced by the attractions of exciting pastures new, nor to be carried
off reluctantly by the force of novel arguments. I believe that whatever
uncertainties surround the method (and they should not be minimised), it
does work and has led to real results. But there are other fields to enter,
and those who question the emphasis on attribution are right to point to
other pressing needs that should be addressed: distribution, contexts of use,
meaning and interpretation.

BACKGROUND READING

The work on connoisseurship is very extensive; the fact that much of the direction of the study, especially of Athenian vases, over the last hundred years has been towards attribution speaks for itself. Beazley himself provided little explanation of his reasons for individual attributions, though there are some in his earlier articles when he was demonstrating the method (Beazley 1910; 1911; 1912; 1913; 1914a; 1914b; 1922; 1927; cf. Kurtz and Beazley 1983: 11–16). Since his death, a number of scholars have set about the task of explaining the method and showing the way forward (Robertson 1976; 1985; 1989; 1991; 1992a and b; Kurtz 1985b). A more wide-ranging defence of attribution (with supporting and adverse comments attached by scholars in the field) is Morris 1993. For a selection of the opinions that reject the connoisseurship approach, see Hoffmann 1979; Vickers 1985; Beard 1991. On Morelli, see Wind 1963: 35–51; Wollheim 1974: 177–201; Maginnis 1990. For aspects of Beazley's career, see Ashmole 1970/1985; von Bothmer 1985b.

CHAPTER V

'WHAT MEN OR GODS ARE THESE?'

In the last chapter we examined the extent to which study of vase-painting over the past century has been concentrated on the matter of connoisseurship – that is, the attribution of vases to individual painters on the basis of personal style. We saw that such attribution can be attempted on decorated pottery, no matter where or when made nor of what quality, provided that there are enough diagnostic signs on which to base an attribution. We also recognised how meticulous such study needed to be and what a complex structure has been erected, particularly in the matter of Athenian red-figure and black-figure for the three centuries of their production. Of course, any attribution can be challenged and, as we saw, the validity of such a method has been questioned, together with the emphasis that has been placed upon it.

It would be a mistake to assume that all the scholars who have made attributions, and particularly those for whom connoisseurship has been of major concern, have done so on a strictly formalist basis, divorcing style from content. In fact, the interplay of style and subject matter (whether figured narrative or geometric patterning) has been seen as a necessary springboard for attribution, coupled with equally close attention paid to shape, technique, etc. Beazley himself was always conscious of the connection, and his most accomplished followers have been careful to adhere to his lead.

Now that a framework of painters and potters has been constructed (whether accepted in particular or not) and now that it provides a grid of chronological connections, more attention is once again being paid to subject matter, to the various images. And some of the new approaches have begun to divorce stylistic considerations from the study of content. It has recently been claimed that 'Image-making and iconography ... leave the attribution of a pot a marginal issue, if not entirely irrelevant' (Beard 1986: 1013). Whether we agree with this or not (and I myself think there is a great danger in considering attribution an irrelevance to the study of image-making), it is time to turn the spotlight on the images – divine, heroic, human and fantastic – in the variety of contexts in which they are presented. We have

men and women, children, animals, and monsters, as well as the pantheon of deities; scenes from the heroic past of a mythological age and of the human race in all its aspects – at war and at home, in the palaestra or in the women's quarters of their houses, at religious festivals or at banquets.

(von Bothmer 1987: 187)

I toyed with a different title for this chapter: not John Keats and his 'Grecian Urn' (in itself a different subject altogether), but William Wordsworth and his 'Solitary Reaper':

Will no-one tell me what she sings? –
Perhaps the plaintive numbers flow
For old, unhappy far-off things,
And battles long ago:
Or is it some more humble lay,
Familiar matter of today?
Some natural sorrow, loss or pain
That has been, and may be again?

The 'old, unhappy far-off things' and the 'familiar matter of today' have been seen as helpful, if not entirely appropriate, divisions in studying the subject matter of Greek vase-painting – sometimes described in rough shorthand as 'myth' and 'reality'. But the subject matter is too complex and bewildering in its variety and too subtle in its meaning to be confined within two such simple terms, particularly as they set up an opposition that is in essence false and ultimately distracting.

There are a number of questions that face the student when looking at the variety of images: What and who are they? What and whom were they for? What prompted the choice of subjects? What connections were there between the myths presented in the images and those handed down in literature? Why is one episode popular here and now and not there or then? At what level would a Greek have understood the images? How knowledgeable should we imagine him/her to have been? Were the images merely decorative or was there some deeper meaning to them that would have been understood by the people of the time, though not easy for us to uncover? What of the different way in which an Athenian, a Corinthian, a Spartan or an Etruscan might have interpreted the image? And what of the differences between the mythology on the vases and on the other media (sculpture, metalwork, gems, etc.)?

Let us first briefly remind ourselves of the range of images on painted pottery. We have killing, brutality and heroism in the martial encounters of legend (Wordsworth's 'old unhappy far-off things, / And battles long ago', cf. Figure II: 1) and the everyday life of contemporary Greece with women at their toilette over a laver, etc. ('familiar matter of today', cf. Figures III: 9 and V: 14). We have the tremendous story from the beginning of the world of the birth of the goddess Athena (Schefold 1978:

Figure V: 1 Athenian black-figure cup, from Vulci, *c.* 540 BC. Ht of figures 4 cm.

12–20; 1992: 7–16; Gantz 1993: 51–2, 83; *LIMC* s.v. Athena nos. 343–80) from the head of Zeus (Figure V: 1) painted in small compass on the lip of an Athenian cup – sixth-century painters saw no lèse-majesté in representing Zeus in undignified labour pangs. By contrast, the humble wedding procession of a neighbour down the road is to be found on a variety of shapes (Oakley and Sinos 1993). We also have the mighty hero, Herakles (Figure V: 2), bringing down the Stymphalian birds (Schefold 1978: 102–3; 1992: 109 'pest-control officer'; Gantz 1993: 393–4; *LIMC* s.v. Herakles V F): here the Athenian painter has not shown the birds as monsters; they most resemble swans, and Herakles, who in earlier literature had merely driven the birds away, is here shown killing them, not with arrows or club but with the more useful sling. Or we might look at a knock-about comic scene (Figure V: 3) with which a South Italian painter decorated a calyx-krater in the fourth century; the costumes and the masks betray a connection with theatre (Trendall 1991; Green 1994b; Green and Handley 1995): are we looking at a scene from local farce in Paestum or does the scene reflect a production of a comedy imported from Athens (Taplin 1993)?

Figure V: 2 Athenian black-figure amphora, from Vulci, *c.* 550 BC.
Ht 40.9 cm.

MATCHING SUBJECT MATTER TO SHAPE

Let us enter this crowded world by an easy route. Some vases carry scenes
that are related to the function of the shape of vase on which they are painted:
they tell you pictorially to what use the shape was put. Indeed the very introduction of narrative scenes has been traced, rightly or wrongly (Coldstream
1991), to the funerary subjects on eighth-century Athenian vases that stood
over the tombs or were set beside the body in the grave itself – such scenes
as the *prothesis* (e.g. Figure I: 1), the laying out of the body with the mourners
around, wafting branches, perhaps to keep the flies away. The shroud is
shown free of the figure so that the body can be seen for what it is. There
was also the *ekphora*, the removal of the body on a cart to the cemetery, or
maybe references to the battle that had claimed the life of the dead man.
Later, the Athenian white-ground lekythoi of the fifth century that were
placed in the grave or on the steps of the tomb also made direct or indirect
reference to death and the world beyond: the soldier husband, now dead,

Figure V: 3 Paestan red-figure calyx-krater, from S. Agata, near Nola,
c. 350–340 BC. Ht 39.5 cm.

next to his wife at home (Figure I: 12); the dead at their tomb (one thinks of
Wordsworth's 'some natural sorrow, loss or pain'). Or non-human figures
are introduced: Hermes conducts the dead woman to Charon in his boat on
the Styx, whilst ghosts flutter and squeak around the trio (Boardman 1989a:
figure 255). We have also seen Sleep and Death carrying off the dead
Sarpedon (cf. Figure II: 1), and this theme too is to be found on white-ground
lekythoi (Boardman 1989a: figures 271and 275).

Another instance of this match between subject and function can be seen
on the black-figure amphorae given as containers of prize oil for victory
in the games at Athens: the patroness Athena on one side (e.g. Figure II:
16) and on the reverse an illustration of the event, whether running,
wrestling (e.g. Figure V: 4), chariot-racing or the like. Other shapes can be
seen to carry scenes that relate to the basic function of the shape, such as
fountain scenes on water jars (Dunkley 1935–6; cf. Ginouvès 1962), wedding
scenes on lidded bowls (Oakley and Sinos 1993), symposia on cups similar

Figure V: 4 Athenian black-figure Panathenaic prize amphora,
c. 480–470 BC. Ht 62.2 cm.

in shape to those used at the drinking parties (Lissarrague 1990a; Murray 1990a). As with their references to the afterlife, the image-makers would sometimes use mythical prototypes by which to make allusion to an everyday occasion, as with the epinetron showing the faithful wife Alcestis, like 'Griselda patient and kind', awaiting her nuptials on the knee-guard that alluded to the homely task of wool-making (Figure III: 4).

However, this simple matching of scenes to shapes is not common and is of only limited assistance. The straightforward, what one might call 'one-to-one', picture soon becomes blurred and complicated. The varied types of images and their profusion make trees of the wood. Let us look at some old and some new ways of trying to understand what the painters were about.

THE TRADITIONAL APPROACH

Let us start with the myths and with the traditional approach that has been pursued. This has been essentially to accept the myths *qua* myths and to seek to understand the image through reference to what we know from literature (see *LIMC* for a fully illustrated dictionary of classical myths, arranged by personal names).

Figure V: 5 presents a Caeretan hydria, made *c.* 530 BC by a Greek resident in Etruria, and it shows two human figures grappling with a monster with many necks and heads (Hemelrijk 1984: no. 23). It is impossible not to interpret the action from our knowledge of the story in literature: this is of course Herakles busied with one of his labours. He, together with his

Figure V: 5 Caeretan hydria, *c.* 530 BC. Ht 44.6 cm.

young assistant Iolaos, is struggling to kill the Hydra which lived in a swamp near Lerna and terrorised the countryside around (Schefold 1992: 100–2; Gantz 1993: 384–6). This painter has given the monster nine heads, alternately red and black, and has alluded to Herakles' use of flame to cauterise the decapitated stumps (hence the fire on the left). A crab is present, sent by Hera to impede the hero's progress. The image is popular in the Archaic period and is found in sculpture and on decorative metal-work as well as on vases (Brommer 1973: 207–8; Amandry and Amyx 1982; Amyx 1983: 45–9; Cohen 1994: 711; *LIMC* s.v. Herakles V C). This vase-painting gives us one out of a number of images that show this scene: it is a stage in the development of the illustrated story, just as the literary references to it give their stages. Hesiod, who identifies the monster as female (*Theogony* 313–18), makes no mention of a multiplicity of heads nor of the use of fire which is first found in the composition before us. So, we can use the information from literature and from visual imagery to trace the development of the story from the images and legends in the Near East from where it originated, to build up a picture of its varying popularity and the differences in detail that arose from differences of time and place, for the myths were never inert. This is, if you like, the rational, intellectual approach to myth. The images are treated as separate from the medium and the shapes of the pottery; they are viewed as incidents, as isolated episodes. They form part of the study of mythology, not of vase-painting.

Figure V: 6 is another example: Odysseus and the Sirens on an Athenian stamnos made *c.* 480 BC. We know this story best and earliest from Homer's *Odyssey* (XII.39–54) when Circe tells Odysseus:

> First you will come to the Sirens; they enchant all mortals who approach them. If in ignorance a man draws near and hears the sound of the Sirens, he will never find his wife or little children standing near him and delighting at his homecoming; but with their shrill tones the Sirens will bewitch him, as they sit in a meadow. Men's rotting corpses lie in heaps around them, and the skin shrivels on their bones. You must row past there; and knead sweet wax and stop up the ears of all your crew, so that none of the others may hear the song. But if you yourself wish to hear it, then have them bind you both hand and foot in the swift ship, as you stand upright against the mast-stay, with the rope-ends tied to the mast itself; so you may take delight in hearing the two Sirens' voices [v. 52]. If you implore your crew and beg them to untie you, then they must bind you fast with more bonds again.

One might first of all think that the painter was 'illustrating' the text (for the story, see Gantz 1993: 708–9), but there are problems. Homer does not describe them as half-woman half-bird; that is a visual image, again

Figure V: 6 Athenian red-figure stamnos, from Vulci, *c.* 480 BC.
Ht 34.6 cm.

borrowed from the Near East (Heubeck and Hoekstra 1989: 119). They
have an existence, as it were, outside and before they appear in the Odysseus
story. Homer sings of them as charming but dangerous women, Sirens
indeed, but in folklore they were also woman-headed birds that were
demons of the underworld (Page 1972: 83–91; Heubeck and Hoekstra 1989:
118–20). Homer also speaks in verse 52 of two Sirens: elsewhere they are
plural; on the vase there are three. And the meadow has become rocks.
One detail is of particular interest: the Siren taking a nose-dive is plum-
meting to her death (the eyes are closed), because she has failed to lure the
sailors on to the rocks (Arafat 1990: 1). This is a detail we first meet much

later in the literature, long after the vase-painting; it is not in Homer but must already have been in some version of the story by the fifth century. But there is much that is not in Homer or other literature, and conversely much in literature that makes no appearance, and can make no appearance, in art. (For Odysseus and the Sirens in art, see Touchefeu-Meynier 1968; Brommer 1973: 441–3; 1983: 83–8; Schefold 1966: 96; 1978: 267–8; 1989: 342–3; 1992: 298–300; 1993: 164–5, 338–9; Buitron *et al.* 1992: 108–24; *LIMC* s.v. Odysseus nos. 150–89.)

It is inevitable that students of Greek imagery in pottery will bring their prior knowledge of Greek myth to the task of interpretation. However, the distinction between visual images on pottery (or of course on other media: we must not forget that there is a great range of other media that carried similar, though not precisely identical, visual images) and the literary versions has recently been emphasised. Images are not dependent on texts; there are two grids of evidence. 'It is not enough to treat artefacts as potential or actual fragments of poetry' (Davies 1986: 111). What is worse, there is a danger that the very existence of a literary version will beguile us into linking the images with that particular version (Shapiro 1994). There is often no direct link that we can establish; there was not one extant version only that shared the same story with the images. Indeed, the visual images are now felt to be separate from texts and mainly based on the tales that were handed down orally, even during the literate periods. We must beware of assuming that painters, even if they could read, had access to written texts; in fact, the concept of a written text is anachronistic for our period. Stories would have been learnt at grandmother's knee, or at the public recitations given by visiting bards, or in the theatre whether as choral songs or dramatic presentations – but there are problems here also. The dramatic versions tended to be sophisticated and innovative remodellings of the old legends, and it is doubtful how far painters would follow these novel treatments (Green 1994b). Also, of course, the painters fed off their own pictorial tradition, 'in house' as it were.

As we saw with details of the Siren picture, there are elements which we know only through later literary versions that have survived. Sometimes none of the story is known to us in literary form until long after it has appeared in a visual version. One example is the story of Talos, the bronze giant of Crete (Gantz 1993: 364–5). We connect the tale with Jason and the Argonauts, and although we know the story of the Argonauts was popular early (Homer mentions the Argo as a ship 'whose name is on all men's tongues' (*Odyssey* XII.69–70), and many of Odysseus' adventures mirror those of the Argonauts), there is little early material preserved (see Haslam 1986: no. 3698). Talos first appears in the sixth century (Simonides fr. 568: 'according to Simonides ... the story of Talos, the bronze figure which Hephaistos made for Minos as a guard of the island [of Crete]. It was alive, he says, and destroyed those who approached by burning them up'), but it is not mentioned in connection with the Argonauts. The most detailed treatment in literature is to be found in the *Argonautica* by Apollonios of Rhodes (IV.1638–88), an epic of the Hellenistic period (third century BC). However, we have detailed images of the episode, 150 years earlier, dated to around 400 BC (Robertson 1977). The bronze giant was said to run three times a day round the island to guard it, and was finally dismantled by the Argonauts who visited the island on their way home. On the famous krater in Ruvo which names him (Boardman 1989a: figure 324; Schefold 1989: 33–6; Carpenter 1991: figure 279; *LIMC* s.vv. Iason and Talos), the Dioskouroi, Castor and Pollux, hold the falling giant who is painted with silver to indicate his metal form. What we have is a tableau with many of the figures from the story in view, including Medea who, being a witch, had beguiled Talos with her spells and caused his destruction. Some form of this episode must have been current in the fifth century BC, but it has not come down to us in written form from such an early date.

There are also a number of instances where there is a total lack of any written evidence (early or late) for a story. This makes interpretation difficult. Let us remain with the Argonauts – this time Jason is the centre of attention. On the tondo of an Athenian cup of *c.* 480–470 BC attributed to Douris (Vatican 16545; Carpenter 1991: figure 277), Jason, who is named, is being swallowed or disgorged by the dragon (Brommer 1973: 490–1; Schefold 1989: 30–3; Gantz 1993: 359–60; *LIMC* s.v. Iason no. 32). Athena watches on the right (Medea has no part in this composition), and the Golden Fleece that the dragon is guarding hangs on a tree on the left. Was this a well-known element in the episode of the Fleece? That it was not a total invention on the part of the painter Douris can be shown by the fact that two sixth-century Corinthian images seem to refer to the swallowing (Kopcke 1968: 282, plate 111, 2 and figure 31; Vojatzi 1982: 118, no. 59 and plate 11, 1; *LIMC* s.v. Iason nos. 31 and 30).

It might be added that, whereas we have inherited one or two literary versions of a particular story scattered over many centuries, vase-paintings present tens, sometimes hundreds, of instances of a myth or episode over the years. It is therefore possible in the case of vases to chart the development of a myth and its episodes through time in some detail: the rise and fall in popularity, the change in detail and emphasis, the local variations, the external prompting that may have lain behind a particular version, the sophistication of one treatment, even perhaps the wilful crudity of another. In one instance (London BM 1897.7–27.2; Boardman 1974: figure 57; Carpenter 1991: figure 23) the sacrifice of Polyxena (Gantz 1993: 658–9) at a flaming altar behind Achilles' tomb was made particularly crude by an Athenian artist, as it is suggested that he knew that the amphora he was decorating *c.* 550 BC was to be sold on the Etruscan market where brutal scenes of slaughter were very popular.

THE JUDGEMENT OF PARIS

It is time to look at one instance of a myth in some detail, following it through the centuries. The myth is the Judgement of Paris (Clairmont 1951; Stinton 1965/1990; Raab 1972; Schefold 1966: 42, 82–5; 1978: 184–8; 1989: 102–13; 1992: 203–7; 1993: 127–30, 288–90; Gantz 1993: 567–71; Woodford 1993: 17–22; *LIMC* s.v. Paridis Iudicium), and we will concentrate on a selection of texts and vase-paintings in chronological order. The earliest occurrence of the story is in Homer, where at the end of the *Iliad* the only reference to the judgement makes a telling contrast between the continuing hatred of the deities and the pity that Achilles will bestow on Priam in granting him his son's body (Davies 1981; Richardson 1993: 276–9). It has just been suggested (*Iliad* XXIV.23–4) that Hermes should steal Hector's corpse from Achilles' tent, but we read:

> This was approved by all the other gods but not by Hera or Poseidon or the bright-eyed girl [Athena]. They maintained the hatred they had had from the beginning for sacred Ilios and Priam and his people, because of the blind folly of Alexandros [Paris], who had found fault with the [other two] goddesses when they came to his inner court-yard, and chose the one who offered him dangerous lust.
>
> (XXIV.25–30)

A more circumstantial account was given in the *Cypria* which is lost apart from fragments and a summary (Davies 1988: 30–2; 1989: 33–52). At the feast for the wedding of Peleus and Thetis, Eris (Strife), sent by Zeus, stirred up trouble and started a quarrel between Athena, Hera and Aphrodite as to who was fairest. Zeus ordered Hermes to take them off to Alexandros/ Paris, the son of Priam, on Mount Ida to ask him to make the decision. Aphrodite offered Paris union with Helen. There are many folktale elements in the story: the uninvited wicked fairy, the beauty competition, the prize, the prince as herdsman, etc. (Stinton 1965/1990: 5–7/20–2). The date of the *Cypria* has been variously set but is unlikely to be earlier than the second half of the sixth century (Davies 1989: 3–5).

We meet detailed versions of the story in various media including painted pottery prior to the date of the *Cypria*, first on a polychrome jug made in Corinth *c.* 640 BC (Figure V: 7); it was obviously an old story, handed down by word of mouth. The scene, one of many on the jug, is under the handle; it is very fragmentary but preserves enough. Al[exand]ros (Paris) stands at the left and is approached by a missing figure who, the tip of the caduceus tells us, must be the messenger god Hermes. On the right are parts of three goddesses whose names are partially preserved (Athanaia, Aphrod[ita]). They are physically undifferentiated – they all have the same long hair and headdress – but carry different attributes. The scene also decorated the inscribed chest of Kypselos that Pausanias,

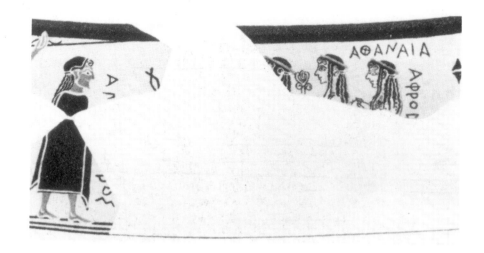

Figure V: 7 Protocorinthian olpe, from Veii, *c.* 640 BC. Ht of vase 26.2 cm.

traveller and writer, saw at Olympia (*Description of Greece* Book V.19.5; Schefold 1966: 74–5; 1993: 190–4) and the throne that he saw at Amyklai (*Description of Greece* Book III.18.12; Pipili 1987: 80–2), dating from the sixth century and both lost. A number of simple and lively scenes painted in Athens in the sixth century show a different composition from the Corinthian of a century earlier (e.g. Carpenter 1991: figure 290; cf. Shapiro 1989a: 24–30). The three goddesses are no longer undifferentiated clones, and their epiphany has caused consternation in Paris who, like any sensible man in the circumstances, is disappearing fast, with a hasty glance back, sometimes with Hermes in hot pursuit: another folktale element or an innovation invented by the painters? (Stinton 1965/1990: 11–12/25–6). In many cases Paris is shown heavily bearded, and this is found elsewhere – perhaps a nod in the direction of his royal status, which the sceptre or staff he carries underlines. A non-Athenian 'Pontic' amphora *c.* 530 BC, made in Etruria (Munich 837; Schefold 1978: figure 249; 1992: figure 249; Boardman 1994a: figure 7.9), gives Paris the elements of a herd (cow, dog and tick-eating crow) and places the setting firmly on Mount Ida (for the problem of prince as herdsman, see Stinton 1965/1990: 51–63/56–66).

Before the end of the sixth century the composition has changed again, and Paris may be seen playing the lyre, which is not a herdsman's instrument. In Figure V: 8 Paris (no longer bearded, nor standing or running) is

Figure V: 8 Athenian red-figure cup, from Vulci, *c.* 490–480 BC.
Diam. 33.5 cm.

seated on the left, on Mount Ida with his goats and playing his lyre. Hermes is attracting his attention or already putting his request. The goddesses advance from the right and are now splendidly differentiated: Athena with her aegis, helmet and spear, Hera with her sceptre as queen of heaven, and Aphrodite with her fluttering cupids; they are all recognisable without any names by them and arrive in classic 'reverse order'. By the late fifth century when the judgement was a popular episode (Burn 1987: 65–8) the narrative has wilted and the figures pose (Figure V: 9). Paris is now seated in the centre, decked out in what passed for a Trojan/oriental outfit of trousers and cap, his dog again helping to set the rustic scene. The goddesses, who have already arrived, posture in their finery. On the left stands Athena with shield and spear and a helmet like that of the Athena Parthenos, together with Hera who is furnished with sceptre, diadem and veil. Aphrodite is on the right and has already sent one of her love messengers on ahead, and Paris turns in her direction and makes an eloquent gesture with thumb and middle finger – the decision made, the deal struck (Neumann 1965: 16; Burn 1987: 65 – 'a critical, appraising gesture' – and 67, n. 43). Above are Zeus and the Muses, and as a pinnacle to the whole story the Wicked Fairy, Eris (Strife), looks down – a character rarely figured. The sun on the right gives the whole scene a cosmic setting.

Figure V: 9 Athenian red-figure hydria, from Ruvo, *c.* 420–400 BC.
Ht 50 cm.

The theme is taken up in the fourth century, both in Athens (cf. Figure I: 19) and by vase-painters in South Italy and Sicily (Moret 1978). In about 320 BC, a South Italian vase-painter at Paestum presents a dazzling scene with added colours of white, yellow, orange, purple and various shades of red. A buxom Athena and Hera almost menace the poor seated Paris (Figure V: 10), whilst the eventual victor Aphrodite leans nonchalantly on a pillar at the right (a well-drawn figure), confident in her success. Hermes is marginalised.

It is possible to treat the episode as a story pure and simple, as above, noting the changes of detail and emphasis. But it may be asked whether there was any motivation behind the choice at any particular time, and why some scenes have a popularity in one generation and not in another. It has been pointed out that the tragic dramatist Euripides in the late fifth century was drawn to the theme (Stinton 1965/1990), but he stressed

Figure V: 10 Paestan red-figure lebes gamikos, *c.* 320 BC. Ht 55 cm.

the wretchedness of the human condition, with man at the mercy of fate and destiny – the vanity of the goddesses involved men in so much suffering and futile death. He is also concerned to point out the parallel between the Trojan and the Peloponnesian wars, and by stressing the cause of the first, he draws attention to the slight pretext on which Athens had rushed into the second.

(Burn 1987: 68)

The painters cannot or will not match that; for them it is an opportunity for display – though it may be that 'soon thoughts of the Trojan war, and by natural extension the Peloponnesian war, would intervene. No less than Euripides, the painters and their clients would recognize the analogy' (Burn 1987: 68; cf. Moret 1978).

Any modern interpretation raises the problem of the level at which the scenes were interpreted – by the makers, the purchasers, and the eventual owners (whether near or at the other end of the Mediterranean). At a time when the social and artistic importance of the pottery is being reduced, the complexity of the imagery is being heightened. I find myself in agreement with such a statement as 'vase-painters were neither theologians nor philosophers, not literary critics nor art historians ... they were artisans who surely intended the imagery of their pictures (when they thought about it at all) to be accessible to the potential buyers' (Carpenter 1986: xvi). It has also been commented that some of the modern esoteric interpretations of the themes demand 'an improbable erudition for the craftsmen and for their customers' (Cook 1981: 130). Literary theory is not always the best direction from which to approach the images (Goldhill and Osborne 1994b: 1–11).

CONNECTIONS

Although there is a danger in seeing too strong a connection between art and literature, it cannot be denied that a residue remains (Shapiro 1994). But it is more a matter of context, not text. Choice of themes, myth or not, in the fifth-century Athenian repertoire can sometimes be seen to be linked to theatrical productions (Trendall and Webster 1971; Green 1994b). Here an exultant bacchant (Figure V: 11) is dancing as she brandishes the hacked limbs of a deer, and a pipe-player in the long robes of performance provides the music. This is not reality on the slopes of a mountainside; this is set on the dancing floor of the theatre. Indeed, the bacchant is most likely a male chorus man, wholly absorbed into the female character he is portraying, though there may be an allusion to the wearing of a mask (Green 1994a: no. 161; 1994b: 24–5). Sometimes the connection with the theatre is stressed in a different way, not by masks and pipe-players, but by inscriptions. On a white-ground calyx-krater of c. 440 BC (Boardman 1989a: figure 125; Green 1994a: no. 163; *LIMC* s.v. Andromeda no. 5), Perseus and Andromeda (both named) act out their story (Phillips 1968; Gantz 1993: 307–9), the heroine tied to poles but no sea-monster yet in sight. It was not a popular episode in the Perseus legend until the mid-fifth century (see Schefold 1966: 56–7; 1978: 85; 1988: 107–12; 1992: 85–90; 1993: 232–3), when tragedians were retelling the legend in dramatic form, and its connection with the theatre is underlined by the words in the background against the figure of Perseus. It says: 'Euaion is handsome, son of Aeschylus.' Euaion, the tragedian's son, was most likely the actor who played the role of Perseus in Sophocles' *Andromeda* (Trendall and Webster 1971: 63–5; Green 1994b: 20–3). The influence of Euripides' version of the story, produced in 412 BC, has been linked to Athenian and South Italian vase-paintings of the later fifth and fourth centuries (Trendall and Webster 1971: 78–82).

Painters in South Italy and Sicily seem to have served a public eager to receive compositions that showed scenes from visiting productions, as here (Figure V: 12) Alcestis, in a version doubtless based, however loosely, on Euripides' tragedy, bids farewell to her children in a tableau that includes

Figure V: 11 Athenian red-figure pelike, *c.* 470–460 BC. Ht 36 cm.

Admetos her husband and older figures of nurse and tutor (Trendall and Webster 1971: 75; Green 1994b: 53–4; *LIMC* s.v. Alcestis no. 5). Mythological themes can also be reflected through the illustrations of satyr plays (Simon 1982; Hedreen 1992: 105–24), and comedy also has its effect: a newly published late fifth-century calyx-krater (Getty 87.AE.83; Green 1985; Taplin 1993: 101–4; Green 1994a: no. 172; 1994b: 29–30) shows a scene of two actors/chorusmen dressed as fighting cocks with phalloi, between a pipe-player. The scene may be connected with Aristophanes' *Birds* (or perhaps *Clouds* in which in a first version there was a fight between two cocks; see Csapo 1993). Again, as with the bacchant, the pipe-player between the two gives the picture its location in the theatre; it is not a scene purely of the painter's imagined fantasy.

Recently the influence of Athenian politics on the choice of myth has been pressed as an important element (Boardman 1972; 1975b; 1978; 1984; 1989b; Shapiro 1989b; for an overview, see Cook 1987a), and this has been equally strongly denied. Why is Herakles so suddenly and so massively popular in Athenian art in the later sixth century? He was no Athenian himself. Can it be that he was seen as an heroic parallel to the tyrant/dictator Peisistratos who with his sons ruled Athens for much of that century? A reference has even been seen to the ruse by which Peisistratos took over

Figure V: 12 Apulian red-figure loutrophoros, *c.* 350 BC.
Total ht 129 cm.

power in Athens. He used Phye, a country girl who was, like Rosalind, 'more than common tall', dressed her up as Athena and paraded her through Athens as the goddess. This is Herodotos' story:

> In the village of Paeania was a woman whose name was Phye, she was three fingers short of four cubits in stature [almost 6 ft. tall] and handsome with it. They decked out this woman with a full suit of armour, set her on a chariot, and showed her how to pose in the manner that would be most attractive. Then they rode to Athens, dispatching criers to run before them to broadcast their instructions when they reached town. They said, 'Athenians, welcome Peisistratos with good will as Athena herself has honoured him most of all men and is bringing him back to her own acropolis.' They spread this news all over town; and soon the story reached the outlying villages that Athena was bringing Peisistratos back, and the people in Athens, believing that the woman Phye was the goddess herself, worshipped the human creature and welcomed Peisistratos.
>
> (*Histories* Book I.60)

On one late sixth-century Athenian amphora (Oxford 212; Boardman 1972; 1974: figure 225; Moon 1983; Sparkes 1991b: 70, figure 28; Figure VI: 17) Herakles is shown with Athena (as he was on countless other similar scenes), but here she is called (in the background lettering) 'Herakles' girl' – perhaps, it is thought, a reference to Peisistratos' charade. However, some scholars find this connection and other, similar ones too clever and sophisticated: how political were the craftsmen? why should they peddle this story of what has been called the 'brummagem Athena' (Moon 1983: 101)? what possible meaning could such political references have to the widely scattered peoples amongst whom Athenian painted pottery has been found?

And what of Theseus, the hero of Athens par excellence (Gantz 1993: 248–70, 276–98), whose burst of popularity comes a little later? Did he represent in heroic action the emergent democracy of the early fifth century and of the politician Kimon in particular? The academic arguments deployed have been seductive (Connor 1970; Sourvinou-Inwood 1971; Shapiro 1991; 1994: 109–22; Walker 1995), and the use of mythical proto-types has long been seen as a Greek method of reference. The sudden appearance of a myth can sometimes be linked to an event or a political relationship (Hölscher 1973). There are scenes showing Zeus' pursuit of the nymph Aegina just at the time when Athens was compelling the island of Aegina to join the Delian League after the Persian Wars, between 491 and 458 BC (Schefold 1981: 224–7; Arafat 1990: 77–88; *LIMC* s.v. Aigina). At much the same time there are scenes of Boreas' pursuit of the Attic princess Oreithyia just after the Athenians had in their prayers successfully caught the ear of the North Wind in their bid to scatter the Persian fleet that was sheltering at Artemisium (Simon 1967; Kaempf-Dimitriadou 1979: 36–41; Schefold 1981: 318–22; *LIMC* s.v. Oreithyia I).

✮ REALITY ✮

From 'myth' let us move in those simplistic terms of earlier to 'reality'. The dichotomy, as I have said, is false. Achilles (e.g. Figure IV: 5) is every woman's son ready for battle, Alcestis (e.g. Figure III: 4) is an Athenian bride arrayed for her husband. The heroic scenes are furnished with the actual dress and impedimenta of the time of the painting – there is little avoidance of anachronism, even if the painters had known how to achieve it. And indeed it has been well said that the gods and heroes had as much reality in human experience as one's fellow men; they were daily present in cult and in the images that crowded the sanctuaries and public places (Beard 1991: 20–1).

Some everyday Athenian scenes, although making a subjective statement about their own times, cannot help reflecting some aspects of the life around them in an objective way. For boys, there is hare coursing, for men the pouring of an offering on an altar; there are athletic and musical contests, the annual inspection of the cavalry, workmen in the foundry making bronze figures, cobblers at their benches, etc. There are also plenty of scenes that reflect the more relaxed occasions of life such as the symposium. For the women, depending on their status, there is the boudoir and the life at home, or there is the bordello (Beard 1991: 21–30). And as with mythical references to present events, there are occasionally real personalities such as Arcesilas on a Laconian cup (Arias, Hirmer and Shefton 1962: plates 74 and XXIV; Simon and Hirmer 1976/1981: plates 38 and XV) or Anacreon on Athenian vases (Kurtz and Boardman 1986), or opponents such as the Persians – there is indeed a rash of illustrations of Greeks versus Persians after the Persian Wars (Bovon 1963; Hölscher 1973; Hall 1993). The 'Eurymedon' oinochoe, on which a Greek (named Eurymedon) approaches a terrified Persian to sodomise him, has been seen to relate to the Greek victory over the Persians at the river Eurymedon in 470 BC (Schauenburg 1975; Pinney 1984a; Hall 1993). All such scenes have been thought to gain currency as a consequence of the events they follow closely.

Many such scenes can be, and have been, used to illustrate everyday life, backing up or expanding evidence from literature and the actual material found in archaeological excavations; many general books on Greek civilisation depend heavily for illustrations on Greek vase-paintings. However, there are dangers here. We are not being presented with a direct copy of reality: these images are not actual tracings of life, not photographic documents, they are social statements, constructs, symbols; a conscious choice of figures and compositions has been made by the artist. In modern studies of myth also, the emphasis is now usually placed on its social role. Myths were sacred tales about events in the past and were used as justifications for present action. 'Pictorial art is a social product which reflects patterns and valuations in the society which produces it' (Leach in Hoffmann 1977: v). And the myth images may indeed be just as much a real statement about social (including political) ideas as about those of everyday life; thus the two strands of myth and reality should be seen as linked to the society from which they emerge, and neither should be seen as being as open and straightforward as appears at first sight.

Two different words now vie for our attention. 'Iconography' is the study which traces the repetition of images through generations and from place to place (see *LIMC*), observing the ways in which compositions develop and change. The escape of Odysseus from the Cyclops' cave (*Odyssey* IX.420–63; *LIMC* s.v. Odysseus nos. 100–37) can be seen on the shoulder of a fragmentary Protoattic jug of *c.* 670 BC (Aegina 10824 (566); Schefold 1966: plate 37; 1993: figures 168–9; S.P. Morris 1984: plate 10; Carpenter 1991: figure 342). There is no Cyclops: the specific location of the men under the sheep is enough; in the sixth century only one figure beneath a ram need be painted to recall the story. In the fifth century, when the story is losing its popularity, the Cyclops may make an appearance in the episode but is given a sentimental part to play as on a stamnos attributed to the Siren Painter (von Bothmer 1981c; Schefold 1989: 334, figure 297) when he bends over his favourite ram with Odysseus under it.

> Last of the flock came my own ram on his way out, weighed down both with his own thick wool and with me who had devised the scheme. Mighty Polyphemus felt him over and began to talk to him: 'My pet ram, why are you last of all the flock to come out through the cave in this way?... You are grieving, surely, for your master's eye.'
>
> (*Odyssey* IX.444–53)

That is the traditional approach – recognising the story, tracing the history of the images and comparing known literary descriptions with them. It is positive and descriptive.

The second way to approach the images is through 'iconology' that strives to discover the springs of meaning hidden within the images (Panofsky 1939/1970). 'Iconology' also asks why the images are there in the first place. The scenes of Odysseus, the blinding of the Cyclops (*LIMC* s.v. Odysseus nos. 88–99) and the escape from the cave are the surface, the visible façade: what underlying structure can be articulated from it? The structuralist view of myth is 'that a given myth is made up of all its variants, that the narrative sequence and content of all or any of these variants is unimportant, and that what matters is the structure of the myth, reflecting as it does the structure of the human mind' (Snodgrass 1987: 135). So much then for the historical approach and our concern with details and variants! The underlying structure of the Cyclops myth is seen as civilisation overcoming barbaric cannibalism by blinding the giant as retribution: the incidental episodes (the cave, the drunkenness, the escape) are there to structure the deeper meaning. We should not be thinking of any time element. 'Iconology' seeks to reveal the connection between the images and the ways of thought of the society that gave them birth. It synthesises; it does not stand back with academic and neutral detachment.

There is much talk of decoding, enciphering, deconstructing. The images are 'polyvalent', 'polysemic' and must be studied in the whole context of cultural reality: they are culturally determined. A wedding procession such as we find on Corinthian and Athenian vases must be seen also for its symbolic meaning – myth as symbol, marriage as death, etc. (as one scholar has wittily asked, 'is there life after marriage?' (Jenkins 1983b)). The implicit categories need to be recovered, and to do this it is necessary to think not in terms of the myths *qua* myths but of the myths *qua* expressions of social practices and institutions; not in terms of the artist and the moment of production but of his client and his needs, of the whole society in which they both – craftsman and recipient – were enmeshed. Images are not easy to decipher; you need to know the language in which they are constructed.

Let us look at some examples from this point of view. Eos/Aurora, the winged goddess of dawn, is generally shown as a nymphomaniac in pursuit of young men (Kaempf-Dimitriadou 1979; Gantz 1993: 36–7, 238; *LIMC* s.v. Eos/Aurora). Sometimes she is shown chasing the hunter Kephalos, and on other vases she pursues the young Tithonos who carries a lyre (cf. Figure II: 10); on occasion these figures are supplied with their names in the background to the scenes. The choice of this theme for shapes that were designed and destined for the tomb shows the symbolism that lies behind the tale: this is death before your time; you are tracked down and taken at and by dawn, at the beginning of your day. We see two examples of this motif on two stamnoi (which are funerary shapes) found in a tomb at Capua (Figure V: 13, upper row); on the other contents of the tomb there are also images that make reference to death – easy to see are the sphinxes which are guardians of the dead (Williams 1992; Hoffmann 1994).

Pursuit scenes in general, usually of man after woman (Sourvinou-Inwood 1990; 1991: chapters 11: 1 and 11: 2), whether they have a specific mythological connotation or not, can be seen as 'rites of passage', whether

Figure V: 13 Tomb group with Athenian vases, from Capua, *c.* 480–460 BC.

the passage is to adulthood (child to man), to sexual fulfilment (virgin to mother) or to death (living man to dead ancestor). Zeus' abduction of Ganymede (Gantz 1993: 557–60; *LIMC* s.v. Ganymede), whatever erotic overtones it may contain (and these are usually to the fore in art), is once again a symbol of removal from this world.

The god Dionysos is the god of wine, release and ecstasy, the god of drama, the god of the mysteries offering you 'better hopes after death'. He leads his pack of maenads and satyrs in an abandoned rout and in pursuit of wild prey to dismember. Whilst obviously as the god of wine he is a suitable figure to head a scene of merrymaking, it must be remembered that he is the one who possesses you when you take him into yourself in the form of wine. The god is in you, you are *entheos* and a victim of *enthousiasmos*. 'The experience of wine is also the experience of the Other' (Lissarrague 1990a: 58). Thus those seemingly lighthearted banquet scenes may have a serious aspect to them, as they remind you of the benefits of Dionysos, not just in the immediate effects of imbibing, but in the immortality that he promises you. There was always the belief that there was a connection between Dionysos and the world of the dead. Once again therefore a suitable image to accompany you to the grave (Carpenter 1986; Gantz 1993: 112–19; Carpenter forthcoming).

Similarly, the followers of Dionysos, the satyrs (Gantz 1993: 135–9), half-man, half-animal, who are often shown gathering grapes and preparing the wine as his work-force, are also made to reveal the fulfilment of dreams and wishes both in their antics after drinking and in their insatiable desire for the females, even if, given their dual nature, animals are sometimes their preferred sexual prey. They bridge the gap and mediate between the human world and the wild, untamed world by which the Greeks were surrounded. They are fantasy figures, like the centaurs and other hybrids (Gantz 1993: 143–7), but have a serious and relevant statement to make about the opposition between nature and culture (Lissarrague 1990a and b).

The Amazons (Tyrrell 1984; Beard 1991: 31–4; Blok 1994; Henderson 1994; Fantham *et al.* 1994: 128–35; Blundell 1995: 58–62; *LIMC* s.v. Amazones) are also figures of an outlandish concept; they are free, tough and active, using men only for breeding purposes. These women of myth exist on the margins of the civilised world and are the antithesis of what women in a Greek state should be – they behave like men! But this was all wrong: women were considered by men as biologically and socially inferior. The Amazon concept says much about the Greek male attitude to women (as do the pictures of maenads who have broken away from control). In their struggles the Amazons are equated in dress with the Persians ('pyjama' trousers, etc.) and they are also equated in their lack of success: they fight and they fail. They serve as prototypes of the Persian struggle but also as the disturbing other presence in a man's world – the unbiddable woman. They are the Greek man's nightmare: females whom

Figure V: 14 Athenian red-figure hydria, from near Vari (Attica),
c. 430 BC. Ht 34.6 cm.

they cannot control and keep at home. An early Greek philosopher,
whether Thales or Socrates, is reputed to have said: 'I have three reasons
to thank Fortune: first because I am human and not animal; next man and
not woman; finally Greek and not barbarian' (Diogenes Laertius *Lives of
the Philosophers* I.33).

And what of the women of Athens themselves (Beard 1991: 21–30)? The
images we have of them, surely painted by men, tend to underline their
normal place in society. Figure V: 14 is a classic example. The wife and mother
is shown at home in the domestic context where she belongs, and with the
necessary appurtenances: baby (a boy, of course), loom, nurse and older child
(or a brother – surely too young to be the husband, he has no beard). This

is the respectable 'little woman' at home. But for the men there was another woman – the woman outside the home, the woman in male company, the girl who shared his couch at a party. Whereas the wife is usually illustrated on a shape like a hydria that makes reference to the fetching of water for the home but also had a funerary meaning (Diehl 1964), the party pictures are to be seen on symposium shapes, cups and wine bowls of various sorts. The girls play the pipes, dance and serve the sexual demands of the party-goer (Keuls 1985: 160–9; Peschl 1987; Fantham *et al.* 1994: 115–18). Study of the different images of 'wife' and 'companion' can teach us a lot about the cultural divide in Athenian society (Blundell 1995).

So what is tending to happen now in the study of subject matter is that more attention is being given to the meaning, function and cultural relevance of the painted images on pottery. Connoisseurship is becoming less central, subject matter is taking centre stage, but less with the traditional method of dividing myth and everyday life into their own compartments; rather it is social anthropology that is replacing the older approaches that are now felt to be failing in their effect. This change is not taking place without a struggle: classicists do not like abandoning an historical approach to their subject. But the literary level is being seen as too intellectual; the images are considered to speak to deeper layers of consciousness and unconsciousness in the recipients. Or we might say that though the intention of the artist, if we can ever know it, may have been straightforward, the meaning, as interpreted by the general public, may have been much wider and more complex.

BACKGROUND READING

This is a large subject. Recent books that consider the images in mythology alongside the literary versions are Schefold 1964; 1966 (an English translation of the 1964 volume); 1978; 1981; 1988; 1992 (an English translation of the 1978 volume); 1993 (an enlarged version of the original 1964 volume); Henle 1973; Cook 1983; March 1987; Carpenter 1991; Gantz 1993 (Appendix C gives a catalogue of visual representations); Shapiro 1994.

LIMC is a massive, international project that charts the literary and iconographical development of the figures of classical mythology in all media. Useful lists of mythological images in vase-painting (without illustrations) are to be found in Brommer 1973.

For work on subjects linked to everyday life, see the background reading to Chapter III.

For more recent approaches that concern themselves with imagery in a wider context, see Hoffmann 1977; 1979; 1985–6; 1988; 1994; Bérard *et al.* 1989 (and Osborne's review 1991); Sourvinou-Inwood 1991; 1995; Holliday 1993; Buxton 1994; Goldhill and Osborne 1994a (and Tanner's review 1994).

CHAPTER VI

'WHERE ARCHAEOLOGY BEGINS, ART CEASES'

——— .◆. ———

The quotation that heads this chapter is taken from a conversation Oscar Wilde is reported to have had with the artist Herbert Schmalz (Ellmann 1987: 245). Schmalz was just leaving one of Lady Wilde's strange salon gatherings when Oscar stopped him. 'Ah, Schmalz! leaving Mamma so soon?' 'Yes, I have a picture I must get on with.' 'Might I ask, what subject?' 'A Viking picture.' 'But my dear Schmalz . . . why so far back? You know, where archaeology begins, art ceases.' Oscar Wilde made other comments about archaeology (in most cases he means what we nowadays would call 'antiquarianism'), for example: 'As regards archaeology, then, avoid it altogether: archaeology is merely the science of making excuses for bad art' (Jackson 1991: 124). Sometimes he seems to have had 'real' archaeologists in mind: they 'spend their lives in verifying the birthplaces of nobodies, and estimate the value of a work of art by its date or its decay' (Jackson 1991: 48).

In the previous chapters we have looked at various aspects of Greek vases – their great variety, the history of collecting and the modern study, the shapes and functions of the workaday pieces in the home and outside, their styles of painting, and the subject matter of their images. What I want to do now is to concentrate on some of the particular aspects of the study that are of academic moment at present. First, we shall consider the monetary value of Greek painted pottery and what conclusions we might derive from that. Second, we shall look at the relationship of pottery vessels to those in other, mainly more precious, materials (bronze, silver, gold). Third, we shall see what is happening in the field of attribution. And last, we shall examine what the images meant to those who were their eventual owners, whether deities or humans, living or dead.

In these we shall really be moving away from considering vases for themselves (as art objects and art-historical material), and we shall be looking at them in a wider context of use, provenance, transfer, deposition. We shall be deserting the art gallery, as it were, and moving into the market place, the sanctuary and the cemetery.

VALUE AND PRICES

So first of all let us consider monetary value. In the second chapter, we saw how during the last two hundred years Greek painted pottery has been highly valued, from the 8,000 guineas that the Government paid for Hamilton's first collection of some hundreds of vases, to the three million pounds paid recently for two. But what monetary value did the painted vases have in antiquity at the times they were made? Can we know? And how do we find out?

There are few references in the literary sources to prices and wages for anything or anyone. The usual line quoted with regard to pottery is taken from Aristophanes' *Frogs* (v. 1236) of 405 BC: 'you can buy a little bottle of oil for an obol, and it's very fine and good'. The word in Aristophanes is *lekythion*, a diminutive of *lekythos*. What did this 'little bottle of oil' look like? Was it tall and white as Figure I: 12? Or squat and black as Figure VI: 1? Was it decorated or plain? One might also ask: Was an obol a large or a small amount to pay? How much should be put down to 'salesman's talk'? Indeed, what was the value of an obol? What else did it buy? What is its relation to what a man earned? Our one reference from Aristophanes does not take us very far; nor, it should be said, do other literary references.

So let us move from the literary evidence to inscriptions on stone; these are more helpful, as some of them list accounts, financial statements, wages for work carried out, etc. Let us choose one example. The so-called 'Attic Stelai' listed the sale by the Athenian state of goods belonging to those accused of damaging the statues of Hermes in Athens and of profaning the Eleusinian Mysteries in 415 BC, just prior to the disastrous military expedition Athens mounted in her bid to conquer Sicily (Osborne 1985; Murray 1990b). Fragments of these Stelai have been recovered, mainly from the Athenian Agora where they were set up (Pritchett 1953 and 1956; Amyx

Figure VI: 1 Squat lekythos, from the Athenian Agora, *c.* 425 BC. Ht 10.7 cm.

Figure VI: 2 Fragment of the Attic Stelai inscriptions, *c.* 414/13 BC.
Ht of fragment 22 cm.

1958; Pritchett 1961; Lewis 1981: nos. 421–30). On one preserved fragment (Figure VI: 2) are listed some of the foreign slaves for sale that were owned by the alleged miscreants, and the prices fetched: Thracian woman, Syrian, Carian, Skythian; and the average price is over 150 drachmas (a drachma had the value of six obols – so just under a thousand obols). Other columns on the Stelai list secondhand manufactured goods: stools, ladders, pestles and mortars, and a multitude of pots, including second-hand Panathenaic amphorae, which fetched on average three obols. This set of inscriptions and others take us much further on the way towards an answer on prices and wages.

The vases themselves give both general and particular help. The plentifulness and cheapness of clay and the vast numbers of pots produced should warn us against setting the prices too high. Some vases, however, carry helpful evidence that enables us to reach a closer approximation. To take one useful example, an Athenian red-figure pelike of the late fifth century BC was discovered in a tomb in Naples and has been attributed to a painter we call the Nikias Painter (Johnston 1978: 222–4). The scene on the front shows the story of Leda and the egg which rests on an altar. From the egg Helen will be born – an odd story, but you will recall that Zeus mated with Leda in the form of a swan, so an egg was the logical outcome. However, odd story and strange birth are not our concern here, for beneath the foot of the vase is scratched a series of lines of Greek in lettering of the script of the Ionic (not the Attic) dialect. Quite a number of vases carry graffiti under their bases, usually scratched after firing, mainly Athenian vases that have been exported to the West, and particularly to Sicily and South Italy; today they are usually called 'trade marks' (Johnston 1979; 1991b; Sparkes 1991a: 126–9). The one under the Naples pelike is a particularly full graffito (few are so helpful). It gives a list of the shapes of vases that travelled in the same batch with the vase on which the list is scratched. The names are *stamnoi, oxides, lekythia, lekythoi, oxybapha*; and it gives numbers of each in the batch and prices (the letters TI which precede the numbers are an abbreviation for TIMĒ, i.e. price). Trying to decipher the trademarks is a complex business: whose price is quoted? the potter's? the merchant's? what will be the price charged to the customer? But a picture emerges which suggests that three drachmas (i.e. eighteen obols) was a high price to pay for a decorated hydria. The pelike which carries the graffito was priced at just over one drachma (in fact seven obols); smaller pots fall far below the drachma level, some even well below the obol level: you get fifty small *lekythia* (tiny little oil bottles) for three obols (dirt cheap), so Aristophanes' obol for a *lekythion* (the same word as on the underside of the jar) was high, but he did say it was fine and good. It was also presumably full of scented oil.

How does such a price relate to earnings and prices for other goods? At the lower end of the scale, a sailor or a stone mason could earn a drachma a day (six obols); a juror was paid half a drachma (three obols) a day for state jury service; a visit to a prostitute might cost as little as an obol (but might rise to 500 drachmas!). In the Attic Stelai a secondhand ladder cost eight drachmas, a shield and a cloak cost twenty drachmas, and, as we saw, you had to pay over 150 drachmas for a slave – perhaps whether second-hand or not did not make much difference (Pritchett 1956: 277 shows that according to the Greek orators slave prices ranged from 50 to 3,000 drachmas). It has recently been emphasised (Vickers and Gill 1994: 33–46) that these comparisons are with the cheaper goods and services; at the upper end of the social scale the prices are much higher and highlight even more the cheapness of pottery.

So pots were cheap in monetary terms, but could of course be valuable to their owners and to families in a way that had nothing to do with money. Quite a number of vases show signs of having been mended with rivets, spikes and cleats (Noble 1966/1988: 94/175; Elston 1990). Also, some of the inscriptions on the body of cups and pots would suggest that, though cheap, owners did not want to lose them; for example: 'I am Tataie's lekythos. Whoever steals me will go blind' on a mid-seventh-century Protocorinthian aryballos; and 'Kephisophon's kylix. If anyone breaks it, he will pay a drachma, as it was gift from Xenylos' on an Athenian cup-skyphos of *c.* 400 BC (see Sparkes 1991a: 63).

Similarly, in grave assemblages like that of the tomb at Capua mentioned in the last chapter (Figure V: 13; Williams 1992), on stylistic grounds there are differences in dates between the vases, and these argue that some were heirlooms that accompanied the dead to the grave; they had been acquired later or kept above ground for some years longer than the rest. There may be twenty-five or thirty years' difference in date between the earliest and the latest. In the tomb contents from a grave at Nola, near Naples (Figure VI: 3), the gap is again the same (Corbett 1960: 58–60), and it is the pieces imported from Athens that are the older pair; it looks as though the imported vases were handled with care and cherished longer or maybe had reached the family some years after their production.

One can see how the cheapness of the vases will affect our interpretation of their importance in trade and of the significance of their distribution. There was no point in retaining them with the thought that, like Sèvres

Figure VI: 3 Tomb group with Athenian and Campanian vases, from Nola, *c.* 390–370 BC.

porcelain, they would increase in value. Some have even claimed that the painted vases that were exported were merely used to fill up the ship as make-weights for the more important cargoes of grain, metal and slaves (Gill 1991; 1994), and had little or no other significance.

OTHER MATERIALS

The subject of value leads us on to a related topic. We saw that figured and decorated pottery was not the only type to be produced: there was black, plain and coarse, not to mention the stationary pithoi for storage and the transport amphorae that carried wine, oil, fish, etc. And it goes without saying that clay was not the only material available for the production of containers: bowls, plates and boxes were made of wood; there were baskets of reeds and straw, pouches of leather and wineskins of animal hide (cf. Immerwahr 1992). Although these have not survived, we have illustrations of them, and they were sometimes imitated in clay: for example, a clay container could be made by taking an actual impression of a straw basket (e.g. Brann 1962: plate 16, 271 and cf. 272), or a small lidded box of clay could imitate wood turned on a lathe, complete with painted notching (Figure VI: 4). Many other clay vases copied containers made of metal (bronze, silver and gold), and the connection between the two (the clay and the metal) is a live issue at present.

It is difficult to gauge how many metal vases were produced and the centres which produced them (Miller 1993: 111), but the numbers were

Figure VI: 4 Athenian pyxis, from Athens, Kerameikos Cemetery, *c.* 500 BC. Ht 6.5 cm.

certainly not small, as even valuable metals such as silver and gold were used in the everyday life of the rich and for dedications placed in sanctuaries (Vickers and Gill 1994: chapter 2). Few have survived in Greece itself, and the reason is simple: those that were in use above ground suffered the usual fate of reusable material, and were melted down in times of trouble. Also, it was not the custom in the period from 600 to 300 BC, the black-figure and red-figure centuries, to deposit them in the tombs where they could have been preserved. The richer a society becomes, the poorer its grave furnishings: as societies develop, they become thriftier (Childe 1944: 86; Hoffmann 1994: 71). The silver and gold were kept above ground in the form of objects, coins, etc., and were later melted down in times of emergency and refashioned; hence the paucity of gold and silver vases (Vickers and Gill 1994: chapter 3). So what we find in Greek tombs and those that share their practices may be seen as reflections of objects in those more precious materials that were preserved in the family.

However, modern finds from unrobbed areas outside the Greek orbit of settlement, if not of trade, especially in the non-Greek north, for example parts of Macedonia, Bulgaria (which was Thrace) and South Russia (which was Skythia), have been plentiful, and many of the gold, silver and bronze pieces were of imported Greek workmanship. Figure VI: 5 shows a heap of

Figure VI: 5 Silver objects from Rogozen (Bulgaria), fifth and fourth centuries BC.

Figure VI: 6 Bronze volute-krater, from Derveni (Macedonia),
c. 330 BC. Ht 85 cm.

silver and silver-gilt objects from a single recent find at Rogozen in Bulgaria
(Fol *et al.* 1986). This was a rare hoard, buried in an emergency; in those
areas it is more usual to find buried silver, gold and other metal objects that
have been deposited with the dead. Figure VI: 6 shows a bronze volute-krater
(91 cm (3 ft) high), made by Greek bronzesmiths *c.* 330 BC and found in a
tomb at Derveni not far from Thessaloniki in Macedonia (Giouri 1978). It
was the ash urn for the cremated remains of the dead; both bones and
container were wrapped in cloth, and a gold olive wreath was placed on the
strainer lid above (cf. Homer *Iliad* XXIV.791–6 and Andronikos 1984).
There are separately cast figures at the handles, and on the walls of the body
there are high-quality scenes in relief showing Dionysos and Ariadne and
their train of maenads and satyrs – again Dionysos in a funerary context as
we saw in the last chapter. Silver was also added for the ivy and vine
decoration and other details such as Ariadne's necklace and sandals.
  The similarity in shape and decoration between clay and metal vases has
always been commented on (see Vickers, Impey and Allan 1986); more

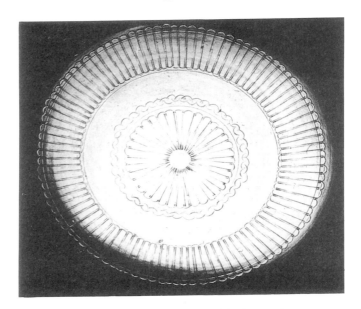

Figure VI: 7 Incised pattern of Athenian black stemless cup, *c.* 430 BC.
Diam. of cup 17.4 cm.

recently the absolute dependence of clay on metal for the shapes has been
stressed. In shape, there is a similarity both in detail (feet, handles, attach-
ments, ribbing), and in overall form; the Derveni volute-krater is a case in
point. A close similarity can be seen in shapes of clay and silver-stemmed
cups as well. We can also compare the deeper, handled bowls where the
silver product is so much more delicate than the clay, and mugs too where
the silver is once again wafer thin (Gill 1986; Vickers and Gill 1994: 105–23;
cf. Sparkes 1991b: plate 8A).

What of the incised decoration? On occasion it is difficult to be
absolutely certain whether you are looking at a photograph of a clay or a
metal bowl with an incised design (Figure VI: 7). The incised decoration
can be found on both materials, in the variety of patterns as well as in the
technical procedures of incising and impressing. The light can be made to
reflect off the black gloss quite as well as off the silver to produce a metallic
effect.

However, the connection of ceramic and metal decoration is thought by
some to go much further than such similarities in shape and in incised and
impressed work. It is suggested that the figure decoration and the scenes
on pottery are actual copies of what had originally been designed for silver
and silver-gilt pieces (Vickers 1985; Vickers and Gill 1994: 129–41). We
may look at a stemless silver cup (Figure VI: 8), from Bulgaria, with a

ΔΑΔΑΛΕΜΕ

Figure VI: 8 Silver-gilt stemless 'Rheneia' cup, from the Bashova mound at Duvanli (Bulgaria), late fifth century BC. Diam. 13 cm.

tondo on the floor inside, showing the Moon riding on a horse; it is of the late fifth century. We may compare it with an Athenian ribbed clay cup (Figure VI: 9), from Tanagra (Boeotia), again of the late fifth century, with the tondo carrying a figure of the nymph Sparte (named) on a horse before an altar. The similarity in effect is striking, though not likely to deceive. In some cases, one could almost say that the incised image, such as the one on the cup Figure VI: 10, from a tomb mound in the Taman peninsula in the Crimea district of South Russia, showing a scene of a man and two women, is just waiting for an attribution to a known artist – it has much of the necessary detail (but cf. Williams forthcoming).

Another technique in decorated metalwork was that of the relief scene. Here (Figure VI: 11; cf. the Derveni krater Figure VI: 6) from the Rogozen hoard in Bulgaria, we have a bowl which carries a scene of the priestess Auge beseeching Herakles not to rape her (Shefton 1989). Some decorators of clay vases used this technique also, adding extra clay to build up the pictures from the flat surface of the vase (Sparkes 1991a: 107–8 and 149, n. 30).

Can it be true, as is claimed, that the very colour scheme of red and black owes its existence to the pervasive influence of metal: that the black-figure technique transfers the gold background and the silver figures to the

Figure VI: 9 Athenian red-figure Acrocup, from Tanagra, *c.* 400 BC.
Diam. of cup 17 cm.

cheaper clay equivalents – those surrogates that were being deposited in place of the more expensive metal objects – and that the red-figure technique has gilt figures against a dark silver background? It is a theory that has been pressed incessantly over the last decade (see Vickers and Gill 1994 for the most recent statement; cf. Williams forthcoming). Some students have accepted it; others have raised objections (e.g. Cook 1987b; Boardman 1987b; for a reply, see Gill and Vickers 1989).

Certainly, the relationship between metal and clay begs questions about our understanding of the Greek world. Is it to be judged on a metal standard? Are clay vases even more debased than our present estimate of their monetary value would suggest? Have we been wildly deluded by the very survival of the clay pots, and the quality of some of them, into giving them an importance they do not merit? And what of the attributions? The attributions have been made in relation to workers in clay, but it is suggested that the very names are rather those of silversmiths, as designers and executants, whose products were slavishly copied by their brethren working in far cheaper material and maybe at a lower level on the social scale. So perhaps we have no names of potters and painters at all! A Platonic cave allegory in our midst! It is suggested that, if we have been all the time looking at cheap facsimiles of more valuable products, those aristocratic symposia and high jinks fit more easily into place.

Objectors to the theory have pointed to such considerations as the presence of preliminary sketches on the pottery designs, 'false starts' as it were, which suggest original compositions (Corbett 1965); the very low

Figure VI: 10 Incised silver cup, from the Seven Brothers Barrows, *c.* 425 BC. Diam. 13 cm.

numbers of replicas that could so easily have been produced from copying one silver vase; the difficulty of envisaging the wholesale take-over of the pottery industry by the metalworkers, etc. Perhaps we may call upon Pindar to show that painted pottery was not held in such low esteem as has been suggested. He makes many glowing references to metal in his odes, but he also has praise for the more humble clay when congratulating Theaios of Argos for his win in the wrestling match at local games in honour of Hera *c.* 464 BC. Theaios had already won twice in the Panathenaic Games and had carried off his prizes of oil: 'and in clay baked by the fire the fruit of the olive has come to the manly people of Hera in richly painted vases' (*Nemean* X.35–6).

Figure VI: 11 Silver-gilt relief phiale, from Rogozen,
early fourth century BC. Diam. 13.6 cm.

ATTRIBUTION

Some of the new theories concerning metalwork and imagery make use of
Beazley's general scheme, whilst jettisoning his principles. The centenary
of Beazley's birth in 1885 was celebrated with conferences and exhibitions.
In England there was a meeting in London, and one in Oxford. The
Oxford meeting was commemorated by the publication of the lectures
delivered on that occasion (Kurtz 1985a). Some were nostalgic; only one
(Robertson's) tried to grapple with the new views and new approaches. As
for exhibitions, in the United States, where Beazley's work has a great
following, a single painter – the Amasis Painter – was chosen as a suitable
subject with which to honour his centenary. The exhibition was set up in
New York, Toledo (Ohio) and Los Angeles (von Bothmer 1985a), and was

followed by a conference at the Getty Center in Los Angeles (True 1987). More recently, an exhibition on the potter and painter Euphronios was held in Arezzo (Rasponi 1990; ancient Arretium in Etruria where one of Euphronios' unsigned works was already in a private collection at the beginning of the eighteenth century: see Zarmarchi Grassi 1992), Paris (*Euphronios* 1990) and Berlin. Both series of exhibitions in America and Europe called forth sumptuous catalogues, and the European exhibitions were also accompanied by colloquia (Cygielman *et al.* 1992; Denoyelle 1992; Wehgartner 1992). The artistic aspect of Greek pottery shows no sign of losing its appeal, and the gap between aesthetes and archaeologists is still wide.

On a more practical level, the Beazley Archive of photographs, which is housed in the Ashmolean in Oxford, now forms the database for the subject of Athenian painted pottery, arranged by painters in the Beazley manner, and the collection of photographs is being extended all the time. It is a scholarly tool of the highest importance. Modern technology makes its archive of information available on a worldwide basis on a computer network, into which individual scholars can tap. In a matter of seconds scholars in different parts of the world can call up the bibliographical information on thousands of Athenian vases (Moffett 1992; Kurtz 1993). There is now also a European Union project entitled RAMA ('Remote Access to Museum Archive'), through which images of Athenian vases can be brought up on the screen through international telecommunication networks.

What has in fact happened is that Athenian painted pottery, being more numerous and more sophisticatedly developed than any others, is now studied to a far more detailed extent than the rest of Greek painted pottery (see e.g. Bažant 1990), and there is a wide gap in the type of work being done on this pottery and the work on the pottery of other areas. In some non-Athenian cases there is still even the problem of attributing a vase not only to a painter but even to a place of production. Take the case of a piece such as the 'Northampton' amphora, once in the collection of the Second Marquess of Northampton at Castle Ashby (colour photos: Boardman and Robertson 1979: plate A; Simon and Hirmer 1976/1981: plates XVI–XVII; Sparkes 1991b: plate 5). It is a superb and elaborately decorated jar with much red and white to enliven the floral decoration and with Dionysos on one side advancing amongst capering and piping satyrs. The other side (Figure VI: 12) dispenses with such figures and distributes pygmies and cranes, hedgehogs, hare and fox around a floral fantasy. One or two other pieces have been attributed to the same hand, but it is the location of the source of the pottery that is still uncertain. The general style of painting is East Greek, and sites on the coast of Asia Minor, islands off the coast and amongst the Cyclades have been nominated as the source. Another likely candidate is in fact Etruria, to which many East Greek craftsmen emigrated in the mid-sixth century to escape the inroads that

Figure VI: 12 The 'Northampton' amphora, from Etruria, *c.* 540 BC.
Ht 32.4 cm.

the Persians were making into their local areas. Indeed, clay analysis, which by thin sectioning and photomicrographs in many cases enables the petrological make-up of the clay to be traced to its source, seems to have removed an East Greek origin from contention but has not yet supplied any positive identification (Boardman 1994a: 239–40).

Non-Athenian pottery has never been studied from the point of view of connoisseurship to the same extent as Athenian, nor can it be so. In the precision, numbers and complexity of attribution there is Athens, with Corinth and a few others faintly pursuing, and the rest virtually nowhere.

Mention might also be made here of a new series of monographs, entitled *Kerameus*, in which all the attributed works of particular painters are starting to be published, mainly Athenian but with one or two others (e.g.

Caeretan (Hemelrijk 1984), Clazomenian sarcophagi (Cook 1981)), and which is investigating not only the stylistic traits and connections but also such matters as individual choices of themes, destinations, etc.

So the flame of connoisseurship may be burning less brightly than before, but it is not likely to be extinguished. As has recently been said of Beazley's work, it is now conventional to make attacks on 'the irrelevance of Beazley's method in the modern context. . . . But Beazley was not obliged to pursue semiotics and the like; had he done so, no doubt we would now be bewailing the lack of a framework on which to place the proper study of art' (Johnston 1991a: 515).

SUBJECT MATTER

Now let us turn once again to subject matter. We looked at it in the last chapter from the point of view of the traditional 'iconographic' study and also considered the more recent 'iconological' approaches. What about the relation of subject matter to destination? As I have mentioned before, there are three main types of destination: the sanctuary, the domestic area and the tomb; and these are found all over, in every town and hallowed spot, at home and abroad, in non-Greek as well as Greek contexts.

Sanctuaries

Many sanctuaries in all parts of the Greek world have been excavated and have provided a variety of ceramic dedications. The Athenian Acropolis has surrendered some high-quality fragments, as for instance (Figure VI: 13) a black-figure kantharos signed by Nearchos both as potter and painter and showing Achilles harnessing his horses (cf. Homer *Iliad* XIX.399–424). It has recently been suggested

> that it was the custom for an Athenian vase-painter at a certain point in his career to dedicate to his goddess a vase he had decorated . . .; that for such a purpose he would choose a favourite shape; and that it was felt fitting that he should on this occasion not only decorate the vessel but make it with his own hands, though he normally confined himself to decoration, using vessels made by others.
> (Robertson 1992b: 132; cf. Williams 1995: 142)

But not all offerings were so grand, and both here and at other sanctuaries small, shoddy votives were brought along that were specifically made as cheap, nugatory dedications. But they had meaning and value for the dedicants, and their respect for the deity was perhaps no less. Brauron, the sanctuary sacred to Artemis on the east coast of Attica, has furnished us with a rich variety of painted pottery (Kahil 1963; 1979; 1983), some of

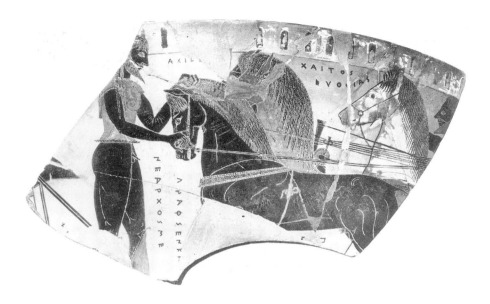

Figure VI: 13 Athenian black-figure kantharos, from the Athenian Acropolis, *c.* 575–550 BC. Ht 15 cm.

Figure VI: 14 Chalice, from Brauron, fifth century BC. Ht 21.5 cm.

Figure VI: 15 Boeotian 'Kabeiric' skyphos, from Thebes, *c.* 400 BC. Ht 15 cm.

excellent quality, emphasising aspects of her worship (wild nature, virginity, death), but some chalices are hastily daubed with naked running girls painted white (Figure VI: 14) – specially made for offering to the goddess and showing her attendants at rituals in her honour (Kahil 1965; 1977; 1981; Hamilton 1989; 1992: 124–7). The quality of the painting is not important; these were sincere little offerings that tell us much about the worship of Artemis and the ritual activities at her shrine. Other sanctuaries have their own special votive offerings in the form of painted clay pots that were doubtless shaped, painted and fired in close proximity to the shrine, to sell to visiting pilgrims. For instance, there is the Kabeirion at Thebes in central Greece sacred to Dionysos, where we seem to see a less serious approach to subject matter. We have Odysseus (Figure VI: 15) racing over floating amphorae and blown along by Boreas – a caricature of an old salt. These and others in the same vein must have had meaning for the sanctuary near which they were made, even though it is difficult for us quite to catch their essence. It has been suggested that they were 'dramatised travesties of mythology' (Buxton 1994: 34; cf. Demand 1982: 120–2).

Domestic contexts

Domestic contexts – houses, wells, shops, businesses – furnish a variety of figured pottery, and can sometimes provide a startling range of shapes, with pieces of a quality to be found in sanctuaries and tombs, though not in such a good state of preservation. A town site excavated in the 1920s and 1930s is the Greek settlement of Olynthus in the far north of Greece, in Chalkidiki (Robinson *et al.* 1929–52). A grid pattern of streets was revealed with small house-plots carefully laid out. The amount of fine figured pottery was modest, though there was much black and plain ware. Indeed, we know that many shapes were made specially for religious or funerary purposes and never appear in domestic contexts. We indeed might ask what place figured pottery, as opposed to black, plain and coarse wares, had in the home (see for example the poor material from the house by the Dema Wall (Jones, Sackett and Graham 1962) and the House by the Vari Cave (Jones, Graham and Sackett 1973)). The preponderance of red-figure mixing bowls found at Olynthus suggests that communal wine-drinking was the chief occasion that demanded a figured vase, but certainly not the only one. Painters naturally included all varieties of vases in their scenes, but it is only rarely that a painter, when illustrating a vase in a scene, paints figures on the shape he is drawing. He sometimes shows the objects smashed, and therefore presumably intended to be made of pot, but these could be plain or coarse pieces. Indeed, it is hard to imagine figured hydrai (e.g. Figures II: 13; IV: 3; V: 9, 14) being taken to the fountain; it would be the coarse or bronze hydrai that would be carried along (as Figure III: 2, left).

An extreme view recently put forward is that the figured wares were made only for offerings, to divinities or to the dead (Hoffmann 1979; 1985–6; 1988; 1994: 71: 'the most important function of painted pottery can ... be described as "the creation of immortality"'). But the pieces that are found in domestic contexts, plus the signs of use and the mends, and other clues, suggest that figured pottery did reach the home. What we must beware of assuming is that homes would be full of figured pottery of all shapes and of high quality, and that clay vases would have been displayed as monetarily valuable possessions.

Tombs

It is of course the tombs, both local and distant Greek, and non-Greek, that have provided the greater bulk of figured vases, and the best. Even if one takes into account the propensity of excavators, particularly in the nineteenth century, to dig in cemeteries, as it was there that the whole and saleable pieces were to be found, it has to be admitted that the balance in favour of seeing much painted pottery as funerary pottery is evident. As has been pointed out, the pots were not expensive offerings to the dead: they were gestures, symbols, and a great deal of scholarly ingenuity has been devoted to attempting to interpret the choice of subjects to fit a funerary context. I feel that it is difficult to reduce all choices to a funerary interpretation (e.g. such scenes as those of artisans (armourers, carpenters, cobblers), farming, etc.).

Let us contrast the destination of funerary material between a local burial (i.e. local to the place of manufacture of the pots) and deposition in Etruria where the Etruscans, who were not Greek, did not necessarily share the values, beliefs, customs or stories of the Greeks (see e.g. Small 1991/2).

First, the local tomb. In the late nineteenth century a small group of Athenian vases was found in a woman's grave of the mid-fifth century in Athens (Burn 1985; cf. Griffiths 1986; Osborne 1988: 9–14). All the vases seem to have issued from one workshop, that of Sotades who signed some of them as potter. They comprise two shallow libation bowls (Miller 1993: 119–20) and two deep handleless cups; there is much fugitive white on them and they were most likely made specifically for the tomb. White also are two delicate stemless cups, one with mother and child in a red-figure tondo surrounded by white (Figure III: 9), the other with a young girl whipping a top; both may have reminded the family of a mother and child who died, and of a young girl who never reached maturity. There were also three other white-ground cups – all doubtless made for the tomb but with mythological scenes and stories. They are difficult to interpret but make reference to mythological episodes of death and rescue from death. Figure VI: 16 shows the story of Glaukos and Polyeidos (Apollodoros, *Bibliothekē* III.23; Gantz 1993: 270–1) in a daring composition that takes us inside a beehive-shaped tomb surmounted by a tripod. The young, dead Glaukos (on the right), son of Minos, is watching the older man find out how to bring him back to life with the herb used by snakes. There is much in this story and in those of the other cups that makes allusion to the nature of life and death. As Osborne comments:

> Placed together in a tomb these vases emphasise the tenuous hold men have over life, the extent and limits to men's ability to control the limits of their own life and to repulse the natural threat of death. Life is won from nature with Melissa and Glaukos [here Figure VI: 16], but nature still strikes back as the civilised arrangements which man learns from nature break down in the face of the threats posed by nature herself. These pictures offer no answer to why men die, and no blind hope of an afterlife, but they do muse, in a very subtle and sensitive way, upon the fragility of human life, and upon the delicately balanced relationship between man and the natural world, between man's ability and inability to control his environment.
>
> (1988: 13)

As I have said, although complex, the stories would have been understood by the purchasers in the appropriate manner – indeed perhaps chosen by them for the appropriateness of the scenes they carry.

Figure VI: 16 Athenian white-ground stemless cup, from Athens, *c.* 475–450 BC. Diam. 13.5 cm.

But what of those painted vases that have been excavated in such abundance in Etruscan tombs? Different values, different social customs, different myths and legends, and a different understanding of funerals and of death and the life beyond. But the Etruscans had a penchant for placing first Corinthian and later Athenian black-figured and red-figured vases in their tombs (Spivey 1991; Small 1994). They even painted them on their tomb walls (the Tomb of the Painted Vases). It is difficult to know to what extent the settlement sites used such vases, as the evidence is much more patchy there than for the tombs (Spivey 1991; cf. Rathje 1990: 280).

There is more than one way of looking at the vases in the tombs. One, that the Etruscans bought whatever they could and interpreted the images in the way most appropriate to them. For instance, the late black-figure amphora with Herakles and Athena and the chariot that we considered in the last chapter (Figure VI: 17) has been interpreted, as we saw, with local Athenian political significance for sixth-century Athens under the dictator Peisistratos (Boardman 1972). However, the vase was found in a tomb at Cervetri: surely the scene could have had no such meaning for the Etruscans amongst whom it was buried (Spivey 1991: 142–50), for what did the Etruscans know of local Athenian politics and silly stories of fake goddesses? Surely, it is suggested, the interpretation they would have put on it arose from their own understanding, and that was that these were the preparations for the dead man's journey to the life beyond (Moon 1983:

Figure VI: 17   Athenian black-figure amphora, from Cervetri, late sixth century BC. Preserved ht 56.4 cm.

109). Also found in a tomb at Cervetri was an earlier Corinthian column-krater (Figure VI: 18), *c.* 600 BC, showing a banquet and a horse-race – a popular subject on imported pottery (de la Genière 1988). Surely the Etruscans would have read the horse-race as part of the funeral games which were usually mounted by them at the time of a great man's funeral, just as the Panathenaic amphorae which were buried at Vulci in Etruria would also have been related to funeral games: not being Greek, the Etruscans could not have competed for them in the Athenian games, so they could not have had them buried with them as the property of victors. And the banquet, whether it showed a mythological scene with Herakles (as on Figure VI: 18) or a symposion scene like many others, for the Etruscans would be the funeral banquet, similar to the scenes with which they liked to decorate the painted walls of their tombs. And if a man and his female companion of the evening were shown on the same couch, the Etruscans would certainly have misunderstood the association and interpreted the connection as that of husband and wife, as on many an Etruscan image,

Figure VI: 18 Corinthian black-figure column-krater, from Cervetri, *c.* 600 BC. Ht 46 cm.

best known for the Sarcophagus of the Bride. You took your choice from whatever the merchant was selling, according to your way of understanding the scene.

However, there was another sort of connection between Athens and Etruria in which the Etruscans created a demand for specially made shapes and subjects, and we find Athenian potters and painters willing to respond directly to the whims and wishes of the Etruscan purchasers. It looks as though the market was worth having, no matter how cheap the individual products. For instance, we find Athenian potters consciously copying native Etruscan shapes, giving them the Athenian treatment and selling them to the Etruscans (Rasmussen 1985; Spivey and Stoddart 1990: 94–7; Spivey 1991: 139–42; Miller 1993: 110 and n. 5).

A recent drawing (Figure VI: 19) has given a useful resumé of the major shapes that fall into this category, showing Etruscan bucchero vases (these were fired black through and through, and sometimes carried incised or relief decoration; there was no possibility of any colour contrast as in black- and red-figure). On the left of the chart we see the dates of the

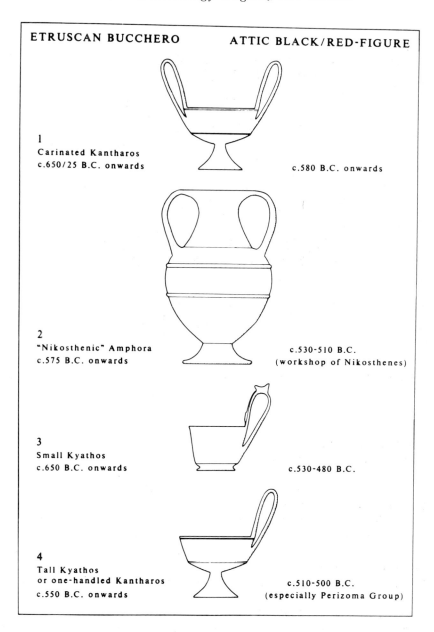

ETRUSCAN BUCCHERO   ATTIC BLACK/RED-FIGURE

1
Carinated Kantharos
c.650/25 B.C. onwards   c.580 B.C. onwards

2
"Nikosthenic" Amphora   c.530-510 B.C.
c.575 B.C. onwards   (workshop of Nikosthenes)

3
Small Kyathos
c.650 B.C. onwards   c.530-480 B.C.

4
Tall Kyathos
or one-handled Kantharos   c.510-500 B.C.
c.550 B.C. onwards   (especially Perizoma Group)

Figure VI: 19 Etruscan bucchero shapes and Athenian pottery.

'home-grown' bucchero, and on the right a list of the slightly later Athenian versions that were furnished with painted decoration for the Etruscan market. There is a further stage in this exchange: the Etruscan potters and painters turned their hands to producing imitations of the imitations (Beazley 1947: 1, 12; cf. Boardman 1994a: 265–9 for later red-figure adaptation).

An extreme example of this urge on the part of the Athenians to provide the Etruscans with their own shapes is to be seen on a unique pair of semi-circular stands (their function is unknown; they are conventionally known as 'celery stands'). Although the Athenians had no use for such objects, they were made in Athens c. 500 BC (von Bothmer 1972; Boardman 1975a: figure 103) and show Iris and Sphinxes, bodies, legs and arms painted in red-figure, heads modelled in the round. Their plainer Etruscan model looks dull and lifeless by comparison (von Bothmer 1972: figures 5–12). So here again we have an example of a deliberate move on the part of the Athenian potters and painters to provide material the Etruscans wanted.

TRADE

Trade in painted vases has become a subject for polemic recently – a 'trade war' is being fought between scholars (see the sharp exchange, Boardman 1988a; Gill 1988; Boardman 1988b; cf. Sparkes 1991a: 153, n. 28). Eighteenth-century dilettanti would not have envisaged the problem, certain, as they were, that vases were made near the point of discovery (see Chapter II). How important were vases as cargo? One group says 'space-fillers' (Gill 1991) with no real further importance individually; another suggests there were less fragile materials to use as first choice for space-filling, pottery needing careful packing and handling. Charts and histograms have been brandished to prove points. Figure VI: 20 shows some selected red-figure shapes at various sites, regardless of date, at home and abroad (Boardman 1979): what differences were there in the types of vases that finished up in Etruria as opposed to South Italy and Sicily? It is easiest to point out the scarcity of lekythoi at Etruscan sites and their plentifulness in South Italian and Sicilian sites; of course, lekythoi were Greek funerary vases, and South Italy and Sicily were crowded with resident Greeks, whereas Etruria was not. On Figure VI: 21 the red-figure output of one Athenian vase-painter (the Berlin Painter) is presented as a pie-chart, showing the percentage distribution over eight sites and seven areas. Two western areas account for over 50 per cent of the total. More work is now being carried out on the distribution of Greek pottery and what it might tell us of trade connections (see e.g. Hannestad 1988; Giudice 1989; Rosati 1989). With the increasing sophistication of computers, statistics are taking a more important role in vase studies, but it should be noted that it is

Figure VI: 20 Chart showing proportions of Athenian black-figure and red-figure vase-shapes found at selected sites.

THE BERLIN PAINTER

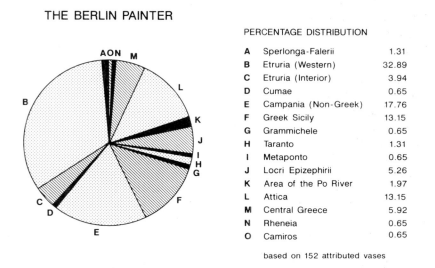

PERCENTAGE DISTRIBUTION

A	Sperlonga-Falerii	1.31
B	Etruria (Western)	32.89
C	Etruria (Interior)	3.94
D	Cumae	0.65
E	Campania (Non-Greek)	17.76
F	Greek Sicily	13.15
G	Grammichele	0.65
H	Taranto	1.31
I	Metaponto	0.65
J	Locri Epizephirii	5.26
K	Area of the Po River	1.97
L	Attica	13.15
M	Central Greece	5.92
N	Rheneia	0.65
O	Camiros	0.65

based on 152 attributed vases

Figure VI: 21 Pie-chart showing distribution of the Berlin Painter's output.

Figure VI: 22 A group of Corinthian vases found at Ampurias (Gerona), *c.* 575 BC.

customary to base the statistics on Beazley's lists of attributed vases, which are themselves only a partial total, and within that partial total the vases that have a context are only a percentage.

The Mediterranean was awash with merchant ships plying their trade east and west, north and south. The main cargoes were timber, corn, metal and slaves, and these would be picked up at various centres and sold along the route. As far as pottery was concerned, it is likely that the further corners of the inland sea would finish up with the poorer pieces that the traders could not offload earlier; this little group of Corinthian vases (Figure VI: 22) was found at Ampurias in north-east Spain, the aptly named Emporion or 'Mart'. As we have just seen, scholars are beginning to look at the material from single sites in relation to shapes, painters and subjects, or at the distribution from one centre and the changing lines of connection in different parts of the Mediterranean at different times. I spoke of ships afloat just now, but nothing pleases archaeologists more than a ship that has sunk and still hugs its varied cargo. In the last generation underwater archaeology has had an important part to play. The vast amount of information that has been won from the sea bed, whether as an indication of the millstones as ballast for the transport amphorae, or the more fragile fine wares by which the ship and its cargo may be dated, is now being made to give up its secrets (Parker 1992).

We have seen how the eighteenth century viewed 'Etruscan vases', how clay was an indispensable necessity in everyday life, how painters have been summoned out of line and composition, how subjects can begin to tell us about the social values of the day, and how new approaches are asking us to revise many of our cherished ideas and look in new directions. Certainly, 'that great curse of archaeology' has still much to offer.

BACKGROUND READING

For value and prices, see Johnston 1979, 1991b. For metal and clay, see Vickers 1985; Gill 1986; Cook 1987b; Gill and Vickers 1990; Vickers and Gill 1994; Williams forthcoming.

The continuing emphasis on individual painters (mainly Athenian) is to be seen in the monographs issued under the heading of *Kerameus* (mostly in German), for example Mommsen 1975 on the Affecter; Böhr 1982 on the Swing Painter; Oakley 1990 on the Phiale Painter; Buitron-Oliver 1995 on Douris. Other monographs that might be mentioned are Bakir 1981 on Sophilos, Prange 1989 on the Niobid Painter, Burn 1987 on the Meidias Painter, Paul-Zinserling 1994 on the Jena Painter, and Aellen, Cambitoglou and Chamay 1986 on the Darius Painter.

For trade in pottery, see most recently Gill 1994 with earlier bibliography.

PROFILES OF VASES

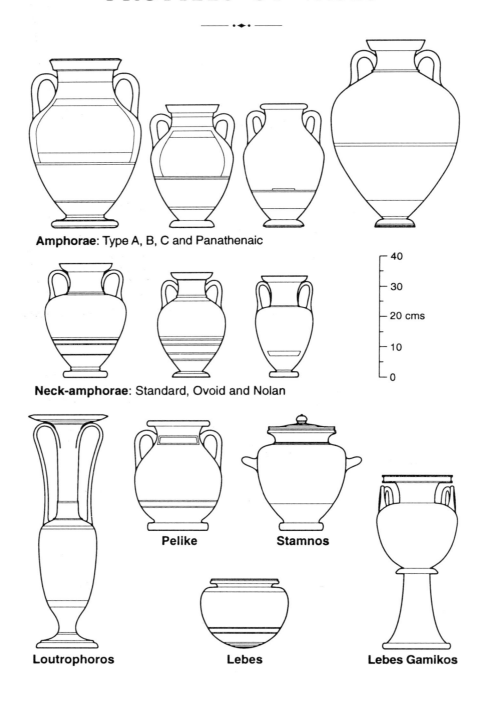

Amphorae: Type A, B, C and Panathenaic

Neck-amphorae: Standard, Ovoid and Nolan

40

30

20 cms

10

0

Loutrophoros   Pelike   Stamnos   Lebes   Lebes Gamikos

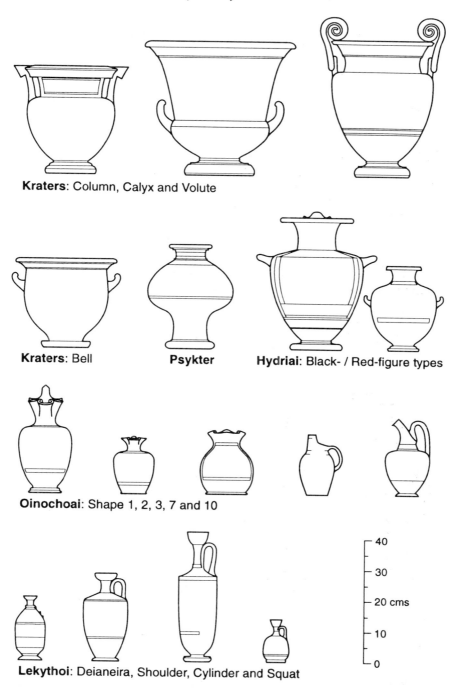

Kraters: Column, Calyx and Volute

Kraters: Bell   **Psykter**   **Hydriai**: Black- / Red-figure types

Oinochoai: Shape 1, 2, 3, 7 and 10

⌐ 40

- 30

- 20 cms

- 10

∟ 0

Lekythoi: Deianeira, Shoulder, Cylinder and Squat

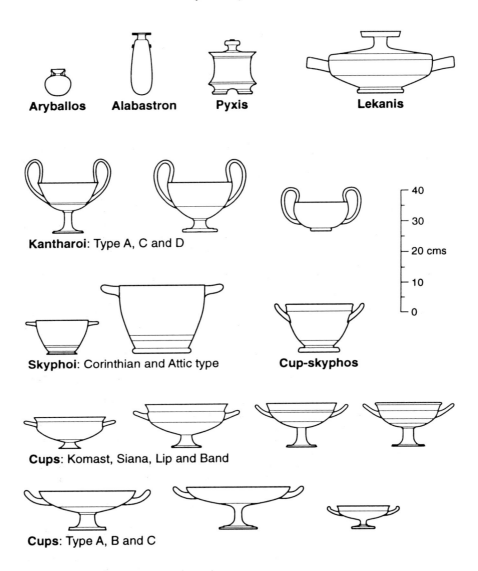

Aryballos   **Alabastron**   **Pyxis**   **Lekanis**

Kantharoi: Type A, C and D

40
30
20 cms
10
0

Skyphoi: Corinthian and Attic type   **Cup-skyphos**

Cups: Komast, Siana, Lip and Band

Cups: Type A, B and C

The profiles on pp. 168–70 are of Athenian black-figure and red-figure vases of the fifth and fourth centuries BC. All are to one scale. The drawings are mainly selected from Caskey 1922; for other books that present profiles or photographs grouped according to shape, see Richter and Milne 1935 and Kanowski 1984. A full list of conventional terms for Athenian black-figure and red-figure shapes is to be found in Beazley 1956: xi–xii and 1963: xl–li.

BIBLIOGRAPHY

———— •◆• ————

Abramowicz, A. (1978) 'Sponte nascitur ollae . . .', in G. Daniel (ed.) *Towards a History of Archaeology: being the papers read at the first conference of the History of Archaeology in Aarhus, 29 August–2 September 1978*, London: Thames & Hudson.

Aellen, Ch. (1994) *A la recherche de l'ordre cosmique: forme et fonction des personnifications dans la céramique italiote*, Kilchberg and Zürich: Akanthus.

Aellen, Ch., Cambitoglou, A. and Chamay, J. (1986) *Le peintre de Darius et son milieu: vases grecs de l'Italie méridionale*, Geneva: Hellas and Rome.

Agrigento (1988) *Veder Greco: Le Necropoli di Agrigento Mostra Internazionale, Agrigento 2 maggio–31 luglio 1988*, Rome: Bretschneider.

Amandry, P. and Amyx, D.A. (1982) 'Héraclès et l'hydre de Lerne dans la céramique corinthienne', *AK* 25: 102–16.

Amyx, D.A. (1958) 'The Attic Stelai, Part III', *Hesperia* 27: 163–310.

—— (1983) 'Archaic vase-painting vis-à-vis "free" painting at Corinth', in W.G. Moon (ed.) *Ancient Greek Art and Iconography*, Madison: University of Wisconsin Press.

—— (1988) *Corinthian Vase-Painting of the Archaic Period*, Berkeley and Los Angeles: University of California Press.

Andronikos, M. (1984) *Vergina: the royal tombs and the ancient city*, Athens: Ekdotike.

Ansaldi, G.R. (1937) 'Wicar Disegnatore', *Bollettino d'Arte* 30: 561–71.

Antike Denkmäler (1887–) Berlin: George Reimer.

Arafat, K. (1990) *Classical Zeus*, Oxford: Clarendon Press.

Arias, P.E., Hirmer, M. and Shefton, B. (1962) *A History of Greek Vase-Painting*, London: Thames & Hudson.

Ashmole, B. (1970/1985) 'Sir John Beazley (1885–1970)', *PBA* 56: 443–61, and (1985) in D. Kurtz (ed.) *Beazley and Oxford*, Oxford: Oxford University Committee for Archaeology.

Auden, W.H. and Mayer, E. (1970) *J.W. Goethe Italian Journey (1786–1788)*, Harmondsworth: Penguin.

Bailey, D.M. (1963) *Greek and Roman Pottery Lamps*, London: The Trustees of the British Museum.

—— (1975) *A Catalogue of Lamps in the British Museum I: Greek, Hellenistic and early Roman pottery lamps*, London: British Museum Publications.

—— (1992) 'Small objects in the dal Pozzo-Albani drawings: early gatherings', *Quaderni Puteani 2 Cassiano dal Pozzo's Paper Museum 1*: 3–30.

Bakir, G. (1981) *Sophilos, ein Beitrag zu seinem Stil*, Mainz: Philipp von Zabern.

Barron, J.P. (1972) 'New light on old walls: the murals of the Theseion', *JHS* 92: 20–45.

Bažant, J. (1985) *Les citoyens sur les vases athéniens du 6e au 4e siècle av. J.C.*, Prague: Czechoslovak Academy.

—— (1990) 'The case for a complex approach to Athenian vase-painting', *Metis* 5: 93–112.

Beard, M. (1986) 'Signed against unsigned', *Times Literary Supplement* September 12: 1013.

—— (1991) 'Adopting an approach II', in T. Rasmussen and N. Spivey (eds) *Looking at Greek Vases*, Cambridge: Cambridge University Press.

Beazley, J.D. (1910) 'Kleophrades', *JHS* 30: 38–68.

—— (1911) 'The Master of the Berlin amphora', *JHS* 31: 276–95.

—— (1912) 'The Master of the Boston Pan-krater', *JHS* 32: 354–69.

—— (1913) 'The Master of the Eucharides-stamnos in Copenhagen', *ABSA* 18: 217–33.

—— (1914a) 'The Master of the Stroganoff Nikoxenos vase', *ABSA* 19: 229–47.

—— (1914b) 'The Master of the Achilles amphora in the Vatican', *JHS* 34: 179–226.

—— (1922) 'Citharoedus', *JHS* 42: 70–98.

—— (1927) 'The Antimenes Painter', *JHS* 47: 63–92.

—— (1928) *Greek Vases in Poland*, Oxford: Clarendon Press.

—— (1930/1974) *Der Berliner Maler/The Berlin Painter*, Berlin: Heinrich Keller and Mainz: Philipp von Zabern.

—— (1931) 'Aryballos', *ABSA* 29: 187–215.

—— (1931/1974) *Der Pan-Maler/The Pan Painter*, Berlin: Heinrich Keller and Mainz: Philipp von Zabern.

—— (1933) *Campana Fragments in Florence*, London: Oxford University Press.

—— (1933/1974) *Der Kleophrades-Maler/The Kleophrades Painter*, Berlin: Heinrich Keller and Mainz: Philipp von Zabern.

—— (1938/1989) *Attic White Lekythoi*, Oxford: Oxford University Press, and (1989) in D.C. Kurtz (ed.) *Greek Vases: lectures by J.D. Beazley*, Oxford: Clarendon Press.

—— (1944/1989) 'Potter and painter in ancient Athens', *PBA* 30: 87–125, and (1989) in D.C. Kurtz (ed.) *Greek Vases: lectures by J.D. Beazley*, Oxford: Clarendon Press.

—— (1947) *Etruscan Vase-Painting*, Oxford: Clarendon Press.

—— (1947/1989) 'Some Attic vases in the Cyprus Museum', *PBA* 33: 195–243 and (revised by D.C. Kurtz 1989) Oxford: Oxford University Committee for Archaeology.

—— (1951/1986) *The Development of Attic Black-Figure*, Berkeley and Los Angeles: University of California Press.

—— (1956) *Attic Black-Figure Vase-Painters*, Oxford: Clarendon Press.

—— (1963) *Attic Red-Figure Vase-Painters* (2nd edn), Oxford: Clarendon Press.

—— (1964/1989) *The Berlin Painter*, Melbourne: Australian Humanities Research Council, and (1989) in D.C. Kurtz (ed.) *Greek Vases: lectures by J.D. Beazley*, Oxford: Clarendon Press.

—— (1971) *Paralipomena*, Oxford: Clarendon Press.

Beazley, J.D. and Payne, H.G.G. (1929) 'Attic black-figured fragments from Naukratis', *JHS* 49: 253–72.

Benson, J.L. (1970) *Horse, Bird and Man: the origins of Greek painting*, Amherst: University of Massachusetts Press.

Bérard, C., Bron, C., Durand, J.-L. *et al.* (1989) *A City of Images: iconography and society in ancient Greece*, trans. D. Lyons, Princeton: Princeton University Press. Originally published in 1984 in French, *La cité des images: religion et société en Grèce antique*, Paris: Fernand Nathan.

Bloesch, H. (ed.) (1982) *Greek Vases from the Hirschmann Collection*, Zurich: Hans Rohr.

Blok, J.H. (1994) *The Early Amazons: modern and ancient perspectives on a persistent myth*, Leiden: E.J. Brill.

Blundell, S. (1995) *Women in Ancient Greece*, London: British Museum Press.

Boardman, J. (1952) 'Pottery from Eretria', *ABSA* 47: 1–48.
—— (1972) 'Herakles, Peisistratos and sons', *RA*: 57–72.
—— (1974) *Athenian Black Figure Vases*, London: Thames & Hudson.
—— (1975a) *Athenian Red Figure Vases: the Archaic Period*, London: Thames & Hudson.
—— (1975b) 'Herakles, Peisistratos and Eleusis', *JHS* 95: 1–12.
—— (1976) 'The Kleophrades Painter at Troy', *AK* 19: 3–18.
—— (1978) 'Herakles, Delphi and Kleisthenes of Sikyon', *RA*: 227–34.
—— (1979) 'The Athenian pottery trade', *Expedition*, Summer 1979: 33–9.
—— (1984) 'Image and politics in sixth century Athens', in H.A.G. Brijder (ed.) *Ancient Greek and Related Pottery. Proceedings of the International Vase Symposium in Amsterdam, 12–15 April 1984, Allard Pierson Series 5*, Amsterdam: Allard Pierson Series.
—— (1985) *Greek Sculpture: the Classical Period. A handbook*, London: Thames & Hudson.
—— (1987a) 'Amasis: the implications of his name', in M. True (ed.) *Papers on the Amasis Painter and his World*, Malibu: J. Paul Getty Museum.
—— (1987b) 'Silver is white', *RA*: 279–95.
—— (1988a) 'Trade in Greek decorated pottery', *OJA* 7: 27–33.
—— (1988b) 'The trade figures', *OJA* 7: 371–3.
—— (1989a) *Athenian Red Figure Vases: the Classical Period*, London: Thames & Hudson.
—— (1989b) 'Herakles, Peisistratos and the unconvinced', *JHS* 107: 167–9.
—— (ed.) (1993) *The Oxford History of Classical Art*, Oxford: Oxford University Press.
—— (1994a) *The Diffusion of Classical Art in Antiquity*, London: Thames & Hudson.
—— (1994b) 'Social life in classical Greece', in J. Boardman (ed.), *The Cambridge Ancient History. Plates to Volumes V and VI The Fifth and Fourth Centuries B.C.*, Cambridge: Cambridge University Press.
Boardman, J. and Robertson, M. (1979) *Corpus Vasorum Antiquorum, Great Britain, Castle Ashby, Northampton*, Oxford: Oxford University Press.
Bober, P.P. and Rubinstein, R.O. (1986) *Renaissance Artists and Antique Sculpture*, London: Harvey Miller Publishers.
Böhr, E. (1982) *Der Schaukelmaler, Kerameus 4*, Mainz: Philipp von Zabern.
Bomford, D. *et al.* (1988) *Art in the Making: Rembrandt*, London: National Gallery Publications.
Bovon, A. (1963) 'La représentation des guerriers perses et la notion de barbare dans la 1re moitié du Ve siècle', *BCH* 87: 579–602.
Brann, E. (1962) *Late Geometric and Protoattic Pottery, The Athenian Agora VIII*, Princeton: American School of Classical Studies at Athens.
Braun, K. and Haevernick, Th. E. (1981) *Bemalte Keramik und Glas aus dem Kabirenheiligtum bei Theben (Das Kabirenheiligtum bei Theben IV)*, Berlin: Walter de Gruyter.
Bremmer, J.N. (1994) *Greek Religion* (Greece and Rome New Surveys in the Classics no. 24), Oxford: Oxford University Press.
Brommer, F. (1973) *Vasenlisten zur griechischer Heldensage* (3rd edn), Marburg: N.G. Elwert.
—— (1983) *Odysseus, die Taten und Leiden des Helden in antiker Kunst und Literatur*, Darmstadt: Wissenschaftliche Buchgesellschaft.
Broneer, O. (1971) *The Temple of Poseidon, Isthmia 1*, Princeton: American School of Classical Studies at Athens.

Brown, D.A. (1979) *Berenson and the Connoisseurship of Italian Painting*, Washington: National Gallery of Art.

Bruneau, P. (1975) 'Situation méthodologique de l'histoire de l'art antique', *L'antiquité classique* 44: 425–87.

Buitron, D. *et al.* (1992) *The* Odyssey *and Ancient Art: an epic in word and image*, New York: Edith C. Blum Art Institute, Bord College, Annandale-on-Hudson.

Buitron-Oliver, D. (1995) *Douris: a master-painter of Athenian red-figure vases*, *Kerameus 9*, Mainz: Philipp von Zabern.

Burkert, W. (1992) *The Orientalizing Revolution: Near Eastern influence on Greek culture in the Early Archaic Age*, Cambridge, Mass.: Harvard University Press.

Burn, L. (1985) 'Honey pots: three white ground cups by the Sotades Painter', *AK* 28: 93–105.

—— (1987) *The Meidias Painter*, Oxford: Clarendon Press.

—— (1991a) 'Red figure and white ground in the later fifth century', in T. Rasmussen and N. Spivey (eds) *Looking at Greek Vases*, Cambridge: Cambridge University Press.

—— (1991b) 'A dinoid volute-krater by the Meleager Painter: an Attic vase in the South Italian manner', *Greek Vases in the J. Paul Getty Museum 5 (OPA 7)*: 107–30.

Buxton, R. (1994) *Imaginary Greece: the contexts of mythology*, Cambridge: Cambridge University Press.

Cameron, A. and Kuhrt, A. (eds) (1983/1993) *Images of Women in Antiquity*, London: Croom Helm/Routledge.

Camp, J. McK. (1994) 'The civic life of Athens' in J. Boardman (ed.) *The Cambridge Ancient History. Plates to Volumes V and VI The Fifth and Fourth Centuries B.C.*, Cambridge: Cambridge University Press.

Canino, Prince of (1831) 'Note by the Prince of Canino', *Archaeologia* 23: 260–76.

Cannon-Brookes, P. (1994) 'Antiquities in the market place: placing a price on documentation', *Antiquity* 68: 349–50.

Carpenter, T.H. (1983) 'On the dating of the Tyrrhenian Group', *OJA* 2: 279–93.

—— (1984a) 'The Tyrrhenian Group: problems of provenance', *OJA* 3: 45–56.

—— (1984b) *Summary Guide to* Corpus Vasorum Antiquorum, Oxford: Oxford University Press.

—— (1986) *Dionysian Imagery in Archaic Greek Art*, Oxford: Clarendon Press.

—— (1989) *Beazley Addenda*, Oxford: Oxford UniversityPress.

—— (1991) *Art and Myth in Ancient Greece*, London: Thames & Hudson.

—— (forthcoming) *Dionysian Imagery in Fifth Century Athens*, Oxford: Clarendon Press.

Carter, J. (1972) 'The beginnings of narrative art in the Greek Geometric period', *ABSA* 67: 25–58.

Caskey, L.D. (1922) *Geometry of Greek Vases*, Boston, Mass.: Museum of Fine Arts.

Caskey, L.D. and Beazley, J.D. (1963) *Attic Vase-Paintings in the Museum of Fine Arts, Boston III*, Boston, Mass.: Museum of Fine Arts.

Charbonneaux, J., Martin, R. and Villard, F. (1971) *Archaic Greek Art*, London: Thames & Hudson.

—— (1973a) *Classical Greece*, London: Thames & Hudson.

—— (1973b) *Hellenistic Art*, London; Thames & Hudson.

Childe, V.G. (1944) *Progress and Archaeology*, London: Watts.

Clairmont, C. (1951) *Das Parisurteil in der antiken Kunst*, Zürich: privately printed.

Clark, K. (1969) *Piero della Francesca*, London and New York: Phaidon.

Cohen, B. (1978) *Attic Bilingual Vases and their Painters*, New York and London: Garland Publishing.

—— (1989) 'Oddities of very early red-figure and a new fragment at the Getty', *Greek Vases in the Getty Museum 4 (OPA 5)*: 73–82.

—— (1994) 'From bowman to clubman: Herakles and Olympia', *Art Bulletin* 76: 695–715.

Coldstream, J.N. (1968) *Greek Geometric Pottery*, London: Methuen.

—— (1991) 'The Geometric style: birth of the picture', in T. Rasmussen and N. Spivey (eds) *Looking at Greek Vases*, Cambridge: Cambridge University Press.

Connor, W.R. (1970) 'Theseus in classical Athens', in A. Ward (ed.) *The Quest for Theseus*, London: Pall Mall Press.

Cook, R.M. (1972) *Greek Painted Pottery* (2nd edn), London: Methuen.

—— (1972/1976) *Greek Art: its development, character and influence*, London: Weidenfeld & Nicolson and Harmondsworth: Penguin.

—— (1981) *Clazomenian Sarcophagi, Kerameus 3*, Mainz: Philipp von Zabern.

—— (1983) 'Art and epic in archaic Greece', *BABesch* 58: 1–10.

—— (1987a) 'Pots and Peisistratan propaganda', *JHS* 107: 167–9.

—— (1987b) 'Artful crafts: a commentary', *JHS* 107: 169–71.

—— (1992) 'The Wild Goat and Fikellura Styles: some speculations', *OJA* 11: 255–66.

Corbett, P.E. (1960) 'The Burgon and Blacas Tombs', *JHS* 80: 52–60.

—— (1965) 'Preliminary sketch in Greek vase-painting', *JHS* 85: 16–28.

Courbin, P. (1966) *La céramique géometrique de l'Argolide*, Paris: de Boccard.

Crane, E. (1983) *The Archaeology of Beekeeping*, London: Duckworth.

Crane, E and Graham, A.J. (1985) *Beehives of the Ancient World*, Gerrards Cross: International Bee Research Association.

Csapo, E. (1993) 'Deep ambivalence: notes on a Greek cockfight', *Phoenix* 47: 1–28, 115–24.

CVA see p. 33.

Cygielman, M. *et al.* (eds) (1992) *Euphronios: Atti del Seminario Internazionale di Studi, Arezzo 27–28 Maggio 1990*, Florence and Milan: Il Ponte.

Davies, M. (1981) 'The Judgement of Paris and *Iliad* Book XXIV', *JHS* 101: 56–62.

—— (1986) *Prolegomena and Paralegomena to a New Edition (with Commentary) of the Fragments of Early Greek Epic (Nachrichten der Akademie des Wissenschaften in Göttingen aus dem Jahre 1986)*, Göttingen: Vandenhoek and Ruprecht.

—— (1988) *Epicorum Graecorum Fragmenta*, Göttingen: Vandenhoeck and Ruprecht.

—— (1989) *The Epic Cycle*, Bristol: Bristol Classical Press.

Davison, J.M. (1961) 'Attic Geometric workshops', *Yale Classical Studies* 16.

de Angelis, A. (1990) 'Ceramica attica della collezione Bonaparte da Vulci', *Archeologia Classica* 42: 29–53.

de Grummond, N.T. (1986) 'Rediscovery', in L. Bonfante (ed.) *Etruscan Life and Afterlife: a handbook of Etruscan studies*, Warminster: Aris & Phillips.

de la Genière, J. (1988) 'Les acheteurs des cratères corinthiens', *BCH* 112: 83–90.

del Chiaro, M.A. (1974) *Etruscan Red-Figured Vase-Painting at Caere*, Los Angeles and London: University of California Press.

Demand, N.H. (1982) *Thebes in the Fifth Century: Heracles resurgent*, London: Routledge.

Dennis, G. (1907) *The Cities and Cemeteries of Etruria*, London: Dent.

Denoyelle, M. (ed.) (1992) *Euphronios Peintre: Actes de la journée d'étude organisée par l'École du Louvre et le département des Antiquités grecques, étrusques et romaines du Musée du Louvre 10 octobre 1990*, Paris: La Documentation Française.

Desborough, V.R.d'A. (1952) *Protogeometric Pottery*, Oxford: Clarendon Press.

—— (1972) *The Greek Dark Ages*, London: Ernest Benn.

d'Hancarville, Baron (P.-F. Hugues) (1766–7) *Collection of Etruscan, Greek and Roman Antiquities from the Cabinet of the Hon. Wm. Hamilton*, Naples.

Diehl, E. (1964) *Die Hydria: Formgeschichte und Werwendung im Kult des Altertums*, Mainz: Philipp von Zabern.

Dohrn, T. (1985) 'Schwarzgefirnisste Plakettenvasen', *RM* 92: 77–106.

Dunkley, B. (1935–6) 'Greek fountain-buildings before 300 B.C.', *ABSA* 36: 142–204.

Eiselein, J. (ed.) (1825) *Winckelmanns Sämtliche Werke*, Osnabrück: Zeller.

Eisenberg, J.M. (1994) 'The December 1993 antiquities sales', *Minerva* 5, 2: 28–37.

Ellmann, R. (1987) *Oscar Wilde*, London: Hamish Hamilton.

Elsner, J. (1990) 'Significant details: systems, certainties and the art-historian as detective', *Antiquity* 64: 950–2.

Elston, M. (1990) 'Ancient repairs of Greek vases in the J. Paul Getty Museum', *GettyMusJ* 18: 53–68.

Empereur, J.-Y. and Garlan, Y. (eds) (1986) *Recherches sur les amphores grecques* (*BCH Supplément XIII*), Athens: École française d'Athènes.

Ettlinger, L.D. (1978) *Antonio and Piero Pallaiuolo*, Oxford: Phaidon.

Euphronios (1990) *Euphronios, peintre à Athènes au VIe siècle avant J.-C.*, Paris: Réunion des Musées Nationaux.

Fantham, E., Foley, H.P., Kampen, N.B. (1994) *Women in the Classical World: image and text*, New York: Oxford University Press.

Finley, M.I. (1965) 'Technical innovation and economic progress in the ancient world', *Economic History Review* 18: 29–45.

—— (1983) *Economy and Society in Ancient Greece*, Harmondsworth: Penguin

Fittschen, K. (1969) *Untersuchungen zum Beginn der Sagendarstellungen bei den Griechen*, Berlin: Bruno Hessling.

Fol, A., Nikolov, B. and Hoddinott, R.F. (1986) *The Rogozen Treasure*, London: British Museum Publications.

Fothergill, B. (1969) *Sir William Hamilton, Envoy Extraordinary*, London: Faber & Faber.

Frel, J. (1973) *Panathenaic Prize Amphoras*, Athens: Esperos.

Froning, H. (1982) *Katalog der griechischen und italischen Vasen*, Essen: Museum Folkwang and Verlagshaus Wienand.

Furtwängler, A. (1885) *Beschreibung der Vasensammlung im Antiquarium*, Berlin: W. Spemann.

Fusco, L. (1979) 'Antonio Pollaiuolo's use of the antique', *JWCI* 42: 257–63.

Gantz, T. (1993) *Early Greek Myth: a guide to literary and artistic sources*, Baltimore and London: Johns Hopkins University Press.

Garland, R.S.J. (1985) *The Greek Way of Death*, London: Duckworth.

Genick, A. and Furtwängler, A. (1883) *Griechische Keramik*, Berlin: Ernst Wasmuth.

Gex, K. and McPhee, I. (1995) 'The Painter of the Eretria Cup: a Euboian red-figure vase-painter', *AK* 38: 3–10.

Gill, D.W.J. (1986) 'Classical Greek fictile imitations of precious metal vases', in M. Vickers (ed.) *Pots and Pans, Precious Metals and Ceramics in the Muslim, Chinese and Graeco-Roman Worlds* (*Oxford Studies in Islamic Art III*), Oxford: Oxford University Press.

—— (1987) 'An Attic lamp in Reggio: the largest batch notation outside Athens?', *OJA* 6: 121–5.

—— (1988) 'Trade in Greek decorated pottery: some corrections', *OJA* 7: 369–70.

—— (1991) 'Pots and trade: spacefillers or *objets d'art*?', *JHS* 111: 29–47.

—— (1994) 'Positivism, pots and long-distance trade', in I. Morris (ed.), *Classical Greece: ancient histories and modern archaeologies*, Cambridge: Cambridge University Press.

—— (forthcoming) *Attic Black-Glazed Pottery in the Fifth Century B.C.: workshops and export*, Oxford: Clarendon Press.

Gill, D.W.J. and Vickers, M. (1989) 'Pots and kettles', *RA*: 297–303.

—— (1990) 'Reflected glory: pottery and precious metal in classical Greece', *JDAI* 105: 1–30.

Ginouvès, R. (1962) *Balaneutikè: recherches sur le bain dans l'antiquité grecque*, Paris: de Boccard.

Giouri, E. (1978) Ο κρατήρας του Δερβενίου, Athens: Greek Archaeological Society.

Giudice, F. (1989) *Vasi e Frammenti 'Beazley' de Locri Epizefiri*, Catania: Università, Istituto di Archeologia.

Goldhill, S. and Osborne, R. (eds) (1994a) *Art and Text in Ancient Greek Culture*, Cambridge: Cambridge University Press.

—— (1994b) 'Introduction: programmatics and polemics', in S. Goldhill and R. Osborne (eds) *Art and Text in Ancient Greek Culture*, Cambridge: Cambridge University Press.

Gombrich, E.H. (1976) 'Bonaventura Berlinghieri's palmettes', *JWCI* 39: 234–6.

Govi, C.M. (1992) 'Le "style étrusque"', in P. Parlavecchia, M. Pallottino, G. Camporeale, *Les Étrusques et l'Europe*, Paris: Réunion des Musées Nationaux.

Grace, V.R. (1961) *Amphoras and the Ancient Wine Trade*, Princeton: American School of Classical Studies at Athens.

Graef, B. and Langlotz, E. (1925–33) *Die Antiken Vasen von der Akropolis zu Athen*, Berlin: de Gruyter.

Graham, A.J. (1975) 'Beehives from ancient Greece', *Bee World* 56, 2: 64–75.

Green, J.R. (1976) *Gnathia Pottery in the Akademisches Kunstmuseum, Bonn*, Mainz: Philipp von Zabern.

—— (1985) 'A representation of the Birds of Aristophanes', *Greek Vases in the J. Paul Getty Museum 2 (OPA 3)*: 95–118.

—— (1994a) 'The Theatre', in J. Boardman (ed.) *The Cambridge Ancient History, Plates to Volumes V and VI The Fifth and Fourth Centuries B.C.*, Cambridge: Cambridge University Press.

—— (1994b) *Theatre in Ancient Greek Society*, London: Routledge.

Green, R. and Handley, E. (1995) *Images of the Greek Theatre*, London: British Museum Press.

Greenhalgh, M. (1978) *The Classical Tradition in Art*, London: Duckworth.

—— (1982) *Donatello and His Sources*, New York: Holmes & Meier.

—— (1989) *The Survival of Roman Antiquities in the Middle Ages*, London: Duckworth.

Greifenhagen, A. (1939) 'Griechische Vasen auf Bildnissen der Zeit Winckelmanns und des Klassizismus', *Nachrichten von der Gesellschaft der Wissenschaften zu Göttingen* 3, 7: 199–230.

—— (1963) 'Nachklänge griechischer Vasenfunde im Klassizismus (1790–1840)', *Jahrbuch der Berliner Museen* 5: 84–105.

Griffiths, A. (1986) '"What leaf-fringed legend?" A cup by the Sotades Painter in London', *JHS* 106: 58–70.

Grossman, J.B. (1991) 'Six's technique at the Getty', *Greek Vases in the J. Paul Getty Museum 5 (OPA 7)*: 13–26.

Hall, E. (1993) 'Asia unmanned: images of victory in classical Athens', in J. Rich and G. Shipley (eds) *War and Society in the Greek World*, London: Routledge.

Hamilton, R. (1989) 'Alkman and the Athenian Arkteia', *Hesperia* 58: 449–72.
—— (1992) *Choes and Anthesteria: Athenian iconography and ritual*, Ann Arbor: University of Michigan Press.
Hampe, R. and Simon, E. (1981) *The Birth of Greek Art, from the Mycenaean to the Archaic Period*, London: Thames & Hudson.
Hampe, R. and Winter, A. (1962) *Bei Töpfern und Töpferinnen in Kreta, Messenien und Zypern*, Mainz: Philipp von Zabern.
—— (1965) *Bei Töpfern und Zieglern in südItalien, Sizilien und Griechenland*, Mainz: Philipp von Zabern.
Hannestad, L. (1988) 'Athenian pottery in Etruria c. 550–470 B.C.', *Acta Archaeologica* 59: 113–30.
Harari, M. (1988) '"Toscanità = etruscità". Da modello a mito storiografico: le origini settecentesche', *Xenia* 15: 65–72.
Harrison, R. (1988) *Spain at the Dawn of History: Iberians, Phoenicians and Greeks*, London: Thames & Hudson.
Haskell, F. (1987) 'The Baron d'Hancarville: an adventurer and art historian in eighteenth-century Europe', in *Past and Present in Art and Taste: Selected Essays*, New Haven and London: Yale University Press.
Haskell, F. and Penny, N. (1981) *Taste and the Antique: the lure of classical sculpture 1500–1900*, New Haven and London: Yale University Press.
Haslam, M.W. (1986) *The Oxyrhynchus Papyri 53*, London: Egypt Exploration Society.
Haspels, C.E.H. (1931) 'How the aryballos was suspended', *ABSA* 29: 216–23.
Hayes, J.W. (1984) *Greek and Italian Black-Gloss Wares and Related Wares in the Royal Ontario Museum: a catalogue*, Toronto: Royal Ontario Museum.
—— (1991) 'Fine wares in the Hellenistic world', in T. Rasmussen and N. Spivey (eds) *Looking at Greek Vases*, Cambridge: Cambridge University Press.
—— (1992) *Greek and Greek-Style Painted and Plain Pottery in the Royal Ontario Museum*, Toronto: Royal Ontario Museum.
Hedreen, G.M. (1992) *Silens in Attic Black-Figure Painting: myth and performance*, Ann Arbor: University of Michigan Press.
Hemelrijk, J.M. (1984) *Caeretan Hydriai, Kerameus 5*, Mainz: Philipp von Zabern.
—— (1991) 'A closer look at the potter', in T. Rasmussen and N. Spivey (eds) *Looking at Greek Vases*, Cambridge: Cambridge University Press.
Henderson, J. (1994) 'Timeo Danaos: Amazons in early Greek art and pottery', in S. Goldhill and R. Osborne (eds) *Art and Text in Ancient Greek Culture*, Cambridge: Cambridge University Press.
Henle, J. (1973) *Greek Myths: a vase painter's notebook*, Bloomington and London: Indiana University Press.
Herbert, S. (1977) *The Red-Figure Pottery, Corinth VII, Part iv*, Princeton: American School of Classical Studies at Athens.
Heubeck, A. and Hoekstra, A. (1989) *A Commentary on Homer's Odyssey Vol. II, Books IX–XII*, Oxford: Clarendon Press.
Hill, J.N. (1977) 'Individual variability in ceramics and the study of prehistoric social organization', in J.N. Hill and J. Gunn (eds) *The Individual in Prehistory: studies in variability in style in prehistoric technologies*, New York: Academic Press.
Himmelmann, N. (1994) *Realistische Themen in der griechischen Kunst der archaischen und klassischen Zeit (JDAI 28th Ergänzungsheft)*, Berlin and New York: Walter de Gruyter.
Hirschmann (1993) *Greek Vases from the Hirschmann Collection, the property of a private trust, London, Thursday 9th December 1993*, London: Sotheby's.

Hölscher, T. (1973) *Griechische Historienbilder des 5. und 4. Jdts v. Chr.*, Würzburg: Konrad Triltsch.

Hoffmann, H. (1977) 'Sexual and asexual pursuit: a structuralist approach to Greek vase-painting', *Royal Anthropological Institute of Great Britain and Ireland Occasional Paper no. 34*.

—— (1979) 'In the wake of Beazley', *Hephaistos* 1: 61–70.

—— (1985–6) 'Iconography and iconology', *Hephaistos* 7–8: 61–6.

—— (1988) 'Why did the Greeks need imagery? An anthropological approach to the study of Greek vase painting', *Hephaistos* 9: 143–62.

—— (1994) 'The riddle of the sphinx: a case study in Athenian immortality symbolism', in I. Morris (ed.) *Classical Greece: ancient histories and modern archaeologies*, Cambridge: Cambridge University Press.

Holliday, P.J. (ed.) (1993) *Narrative and Event in Ancient Art*, Cambridge: Cambridge University Press.

Howland, R.H. (1958) *Greek Lamps and Their Survivals: The Athenian Agora IV*, Princeton: American School of Classical Studies at Athens.

Hurwit, J.M. (1985) *The Art and Culture of Early Greece, 1100–480 B.C.*, Ithaca and London: Cornell University Press.

—— (1993) 'Art, poetry and the polis in the age of Homer', in S. Langdon (ed.) *From Pasture to Polis: art in the age of Homer*, Columbia and London: University of Missouri Press.

Immerwahr, H. (1992) 'New wine in ancient wineskins: the evidence from Attic vases', *Hesperia* 61: 121–32.

Isler, H.P. (1994) 'Der Töpfer Amasis und der Amasis-Maler', *JDAI* 109: 93–114.

Isler-Kerenyi, C. (1980) 'J.D. Beazley e le ceramologia', *Quaderni ticinesi di numismatica e antichità classiche* 9: 7–23.

—— (1994) 'Are collectors the real looters?', *Antiquity* 68: 350–2.

Jackson, J.W. (ed.) (1991) *Aristotle at Afternoon Tea: the rare Oscar Wilde*, London: Fourth Estate.

Jahn, O. (1854) *Beschreibung der Vasensammlung König Ludwigs in der Pinakothek zu München*, Munich: Jos. Lindauer.

Jenkins, I. (1983a) 'Frederic Lord Leighton and Greek vases', *Burlington Magazine* 125: 597–605.

—— (1983b) 'Is there life after marriage? a study of the abduction motif in vase paintings of the Athenian wedding ceremony', *BICS* 30: 137–45.

—— (1986) *Greek and Roman Life*, London: British Museum Publications.

—— (1988) 'Adam Buck and the vogue for Greek vases', *The Burlington Magazine* 130: 448–57.

Johnston, A.W. (1978) 'List of contents: Attic vases', *AJA* 82: 222–6.

—— (1979) *Trademarks on Greek Vases*, Warminster: Aris & Phillips.

—— (1987) 'IG II² 2311 and the number of Panathenaic amphorae', *ABSA* 82: 125–9.

—— (1991a) Review of T.H. Carpenter *Beazley Addenda (2nd edn) 1989*, *CR* 41: 514–15.

—— (1991b) 'Greek vases in the marketplace', in T. Rasmussen and N. Spivey (eds) *Looking at Greek Vases*, Cambridge: Cambridge University Press.

Jones, J.E., Graham, A.J. and Sackett, L.H. (1973) 'An Attic country house below the Cave of Pan at Vari', *ABSA* 68: 355–452.

Jones, J.E., Sackett, L.H. and Graham, A.J. (1962) 'The Dema house in Attica', *ABSA* 57: 75–114.

Jones, R.E. (1986) *Greek and Cypriot Pottery: a review of scientific studies. Fitch Laboratory Occasional Paper 1*, Athens: British School of Archaeology at Athens.

Kaempf-Dimitriadou, S. (1979) *Die Liebe der Götter in der attischen Kunst des 5. Jahrhunderts v. Chr., AK Supplement XI.*

[G.-] Kahil, L. (1963) 'Quelques vases du sanctuaire d'Artémis à Brauron', *AK* 6: 5–29.

—— (1965) 'Autour de l'Artémis attique', *AK* 8: 20–33.

—— (1977) 'L'Artémis de Brauron: rites et mystères', *AK* 20: 86–98.

—— (1979) 'La déesse Artémis: mythologie et iconographie', in *Greece and Italy in the Classical World: Acta of the XI International Congress of Classical Archaeology, London, 3–9 September 1978.*

—— (1981) 'Le "cratérisque" d'Artémis et la Brauronion de l'Acropole', *Hesperia* 50: 258–63.

—— (1983) 'Mythological repertoire of Brauron', in W.G. Moon (ed.), *Ancient Greek Art and Iconography*, Madison: University of Wisconsin Press.

Kanowski, M.G. (1984) *Containers of Classical Greece*, St Lucia: University of Queensland Press.

Kearsley, R. (1989) *The Pendent Semi-Circle Skyphos (BICS Supplement 44)*, London: Institute of Classical Studies, University of London.

Keuls, E.C. (1985) *The Reign of the Phallos*, Berkeley: University of California Press.

Kilinski, K. (1990) *Boeotian Black Figure Vase Painting of the Archaic Period*, Mainz: Philipp von Zabern.

—— (1992) 'Teisias and Theodoros: East Boiotian potters', *Hesperia* 61: 253–63.

Klein, A.E. (1932) *Child Life in Greek Art*, New York: Columbia University Press.

Knauer, E.R. (1986) 'οὐ γὰρ ἦν ἀμίς': a chous by the Oionokles Painter', *Greek Vases in the J. Paul Getty Museum 3 (OPA 2)*: 91–100.

Knigge, U. (1991) *The Athenian Kerameikos: history – monuments – excavations*, trans. from German by J. Binder, Athens: Krene Editions.

Knight, C. (1990) *Hamilton a Napoli: culture, svaghi, civiltà di una grande capitale europea*, Naples: Electa.

Koehler, C.G. (1979) 'Transport amphorae as evidence of trade', *Arch. News* 8: 54–61.

Kopcke, G. (1964) 'Golddekorierte attische Schwarzfirniskeramik des vierten Jahrhunderts v. Chr.', *AM* 79: 22–84.

—— (1968) 'Heraion von Samos: Die Kampagnen 1961/65 im Südtemenos (8.–6. Jahrhundert)', *AM* 83: 250–314.

Kurtz, D.C. (1975) *Athenian White Lekythoi*, Oxford: Clarendon Press.

—— (1983) 'Gorgos' cup: an essay in connoisseurship', *JHS* 103: 68–86.

—— (1984) 'Vases for the dead: an Attic selection 750–400 B.C.', in H.A.G. Brijder (ed.) *Ancient Greek and Related Pottery. Proceedings of the International Vase Symposium in Amsterdam, 12–15 April 1984, Allard Pierson Series 5*, Amsterdam: Allard Pierson Series.

—— (ed.) (1985a) *Beazley and Oxford*, Oxford: Oxford University Committee for Archaeology.

—— (1985b) 'Beazley and the connoisseurship of Greek Vases', *Greek Vases in the J. Paul Getty Museum 2 (OPA 3)*: 237–50.

—— (ed.) (1989) *Greek Vases: lectures by J.D. Beazley*, Oxford: Clarendon Press.

—— (1993) 'The Beazley Archive Database', *Archeologia e Calcolatori* 4: 263–4.

Kurtz, D.C. and Beazley, Sir John (1983) *The Berlin Painter*, Oxford: Clarendon Press.

Kurtz, D.C. and Boardman, J. (1971) *Greek Burial Customs*, London: Thames & Hudson.

—— (1986) 'Booners', *Greek Vases in the J. Paul Getty Museum 3 (OPA 2)*: 35–70.

Lang, M. (1960) *The Athenian Citizen*, Princeton: American School of Classical Studies at Athens.

—— (1978) *Socrates in the Agora*, Princeton: American School of Classical Studies at Athens.

Lang, M. and Crosby, M. (1964) *Weights, Measures and Tokens: The Athenian Agora X*, Princeton: American School of Classical Studies at Athens.

Langlotz, E. (1975) *Studien zur Nordgriechischen Kunst*, Mainz: Philipp von Zabern.

Lau, T. (1877) *Die griechischen Vasen*, Leipzig: E.A. Seemann.

Lauts, J. (1962) *Carpaccio*, London: Phaidon.

Lebel, A.J.L. (1990) 'The Marsyas Painter and some of his contemporaries', Oxford, unpublished D.Phil. thesis.

Leighton, R. and Castelino, C. (1990) 'Thomas Dempster and Ancient Etruria: a review of the autobiography and *de Etruria Regali*', *PBSR* 58: 337–52.

Lemos, A.A. (1991) *Archaic Pottery of Chios: the decorated styles*, Oxford: Oxford University Committee for Archaeology.

Lewis, D.M. (1981) *Inscriptiones Graecae I³ Fasc. 1, Decreta et Tabulae Magistratuum*, Berlin/New York: Walter de Gruyter.

Lezzi-Hafter, A., Isler-Kerenyi, C. and Donceel, R. (1980) 'Auf classischem Boden gesammelt', *Antike Welt* 11 (Special Number).

LIMC (1981–) *Lexicon Iconographicum Mythologiae Classicae*, Zürich and Munich: Artemis.

Lissarrague, F. (1990a) *The Aesthetics of the Greek Banquet: images of wine and ritual*, Princeton: Princeton University Press. (Originally published in 1987 in French, *Un Flot d'Images: une esthétique du banquet grec*, Paris: Adam Biro.)

—— (1990b) 'Why are satyrs good to represent?' in J.J. Winkler and F.I. Zeitlin (eds) *Nothing To Do With Dionysos? Athenian drama in its social context*, Princeton: Princeton University Press.

—— (1992) '*Graphein*: écrire et dessiner', in C. Bron and E. Kassapoglou (eds) *L'image en jeu: de l'antiquité à Paul Klee*, Yens-sur-Morges: Cabédita.

Lullies, R. (1940) 'Zur boiotischen rotfigurigen Vasenmalerei', *AM* 65: 1–27.

Lyons, C.L. (1992) 'The *Museo Mastrilli* and the culture of collecting in Naples, 1700–1755', *Journal of the History of Collections* 4: 1–26.

MacDonald, B.R. (1981) 'The emigration of potters from Athens in the late fifth century B.C. and its effect on the Attic pottery industry', *AJA* 85: 159–68.

—— (1982) 'The import of Attic pottery to Corinth and the question of trade during the Peloponnesian War', *JHS* 102: 113–23.

McPhee, I. (1983) 'Local red-figure from Corinth 1973–80', *Hesperia* 52: 137–53.

—— (1986) 'Laconian red-figure from the British excavations in Sparta', *ABSA* 81: 153–64.

—— (1991) 'A Corinthian red-figured calyx-krater and the Dombrena Painter', *OJA* 10: 25–34.

Maginnis, H.B.J. (1990) 'The role of perceptual learning in connoisseurship: Morelli, Berenson, and beyond', *Art History* 13: 104–17.

Malraux, A. (1978) *Voices of Silence*, trans. S. Gilbert, Princeton: Princeton University Press.

Manfrini-Aragno, I. (1992) 'Femmes à la fontaine: réalité et imaginaire', in C. Bron and E. Kassapoglou (eds) *L'image en jeu: de l'antiquité à Paul Klee*, Yens-sur-Morges: Cabédita.

March, J.R. (1987) *The Creative Poet (BICS Supplement 49)*, London: Institute of Classical Studies, University of London.

Margreiter, I. (1988) *Frühe lakonische Keramik der geometrischen bis archaischen Zeit (10. bis 6. Jahrhundert v. Chr)*, Waldsassen-Bayern: Stiftland.

Martelli, M. (1987) *Le ceramica degli Etruschi: la pittura vascolare*, Novara: Istituto Geografico De Agostini.

Matheson, S. (1989) 'Panathenaic amphorae by the Kleophrades Painter', *Greek Vases in the J. Paul Getty Museum 4 (OPA 5)*: 95–112.

Mayo, M.E. (1982) *The Art of South Italy: vases from Magna Graecia*, Richmond: Virginia Museum of Fine Arts.

Meiggs, R. and Lewis, D.M. (1988) *A selection of Greek historical inscriptions to the end of the fifth century B.C.*, Oxford: Clarendon Press.

Mertens, J.R. (1974) 'Attic white-ground cups: a special class of vases', *Metropolitan Museum Journal* 9: 91–108.

—— (1987) 'The Amasis Painter: artist and tradition', in M. True (ed.) *Papers on the Amasis Painter and His World*, Malibu: J. Paul Getty Museum.

—— (1988) 'Some thoughts on Attic vase-painting of the 6th cent. B.C.', in J. Christiansen and T. Melander (eds) *Proceedings of the 3rd Symposium on Ancient Greek and Related Pottery, Copenhagen August 31–September 4, 1987*, Copenhagen: National Museum, Ny Carlsberg Glyptotek, Thorvaldsens Museum.

Miller, M. (1993) 'Adoption and adaptation of Achaemenid metalware forms in Attic black-gloss ware of the fifth century', *AMI* 26: 109–46.

Milne, M.J. (1945) 'A prize for wool-working', *AJA* 49: 528–33.

Moffett, J. (1992) 'The Beazley Archive: a globally accessible resource database for classical archaeology', *Archaeological Computing Newsletter* 32: 7–14.

Mommsen, H. (1975) *Der Affekter, Kerameus 1*, Mainz: Philipp von Zabern.

Moon, W.G. (1983) 'The Priam Painter: some iconographic and stylistic consider-ations', in W.G. Moon (ed.) *Ancient Greek Art and Iconography*, Madison: University of Wisconsin Press.

Morel, J.P. (1981) *Céramique campanienne: les formes*, Rome: de Boccard.

Morelli, G. (1892–3) *Italian Painters: critical studies of their works*, trans. C. ffoulkes, London: John Murray.

Moret, J.-M. (1978) 'Le Jugement de Pâris en Grande-Grèce: mythe et actualité politique. A propos du lébès paestan d'une collection privée', *AK* 21: 76–98.

Morris, C. (1993) 'Hands up for the individual! The role of attribution studies in Aegean prehistory', *CAJ* 3: 41–66.

Morris, I. (1992) *Death-Ritual and Social Structure in Classical Antiquity*, Cambridge: Cambridge University Press.

—— (ed.) (1994) *Classical Greece: ancient histories and modern archaeologies*, Cambridge: Cambridge University Press.

Morris, R. (1979) *H.M.S. Colossus: the story of the salvage of the Hamilton treasures*, London: Hutchinson.

—— (1984) 'Ancient pottery from the Scillonian seabed', *International Journal of Nautical Archaeology* 13: 156–63.

Morris, S.P. (1984) *The Black and White Style*, New Haven and London: Yale University Press.

—— (1992) *Daidalos and the Origins of Greek Art*, Princeton: Princeton University Press.

Murray, O. (ed.) (1990a) *Sympotica: a symposium on the* Symposion, Oxford: Clarendon Press.

—— (1990b) 'The affair of the Mysteries: Democracy and the drinking group', in O. Murray (ed.) *Sympotica: a symposium on the* Symposion, Oxford: Clarendon Press.

Murray, R.L. (1975) *The Protogeometric Style: the first Greek style*, Göteborg: Paul Åströms Förlag.

Neils, J. (ed.) (1992) *Goddess and Polis: the Panathenaic festival in ancient Athens*, Hanover, N.H.: Hood Museum of Art, Dartmouth College and Princeton: Princeton University Press.

Neumann, G. (1965) *Gesten und Gebärden in der griechischen Kunst*, Berlin: Walter de Gruyter.

Noble, J.V. (1966/1988) *The Techniques of Attic Painted Pottery*, London: Faber & Faber/Thames & Hudson.

Oakley, J.H. (1990) *The Phiale Painter, Kerameus 8*, Mainz: Philipp von Zabern.

—— (1992) 'An Athenian red-figure workshop from the time of the Peloponnesian War', *BCH Supplement 23*: 195–203.

Oakley, J.H. and Sinos, R.H. (1993) *The Wedding in Ancient Athens*, Madison: University of Wisconsin Press.

Ober, J. and Hedrick, C.W. (1993) *The Birth of Democracy: an exhibition celebrating the 2500th anniversary of democracy*, Princeton: American School of Classical Studies at Athens.

Ohly-Dumm, M. (1981) 'Medeas Widderzauber auf einer Schale aus der Werkstatt des Euphronios', *GettyMusJ* 9: 5–21.

Orton, C., Tyers, P. and Vince, A. (1993) *Pottery in Archaeology*, Cambridge: Cambridge University Press.

Osborne, R. (1985) 'The erection and mutilation of the Hermai', *PCPS* 31: 47–73.

—— (1987) *Classical Landscape with Figures: the ancient Greek city and its countryside*, London: George Philip.

—— (1988) 'Death revisited; death revised. The death of the artist in archaic and classical Greece', *Art History* 11: 1–16.

—— (1989) 'A crisis in archaeological history: the seventh century in Attica', *ABSA* 84: 297–322.

—— (1991) 'Whose image and superscription is this?', *Arion* 1: 255–75.

—— (1994) 'The economy and trade', in J. Boardman (ed.) *The Cambridge Ancient History, Plates to Volumes V and VI The Fifth and Fourth Centuries B.C.*, Cambridge: Cambridge University Press.

Padgett, J.M., Cornstock, M.B., Herrmann, J.J. and Vermeule, C.C. (1993) *Vase-Painting in Italy: red-figure and related works in the Museum of Fine Arts, Boston*, Boston, Mass.: Museum of Fine Arts.

Page, D.L. (1972) *Folktales in Homer's Odyssey*, Cambridge, Mass.: Harvard University Press.

Panofsky, E. (1939/1970) 'Iconography and iconology: an introduction to the study of Renaissance art', in *Studies in Iconography: humanistic themes in the art of the Renaissance*, New York: Oxford University Press, and (1970) in *Meaning in the Visual Arts*, Harmondsworth: Penguin.

Papadopoulos, J.K. (1994) 'Early Iron Age potters' marks in the Aegean', *Hesperia* 63: 457–507.

Parke, H.W. (1977) *Festivals of the Athenians*, London: Thames & Hudson.

Parker, A.J. (1992) *Ancient Shipwrecks of the Mediterranean and the Roman Provinces (BAR International Series 580)*, Oxford: Tempus Reparatum.

Paul-Zinserling, V. (1994) *Der Jena-Maler und sein Kreis*, Mainz: Philipp von Zabern.

Payne, H.G.G. (1931) *Necrocorinthia*, Oxford: Clarendon Press.

—— (1933) *Protokorinthische Vasenmalerei*, Berlin: Heinrich Keller.

Peacock, D.P.S. (1982) *Pottery in the Roman World: an ethnoarchaeological approach*, London: Longman.

Peacock, D.P.S. and Williams, D.F. (1986) *Amphorae and the Roman Economy: an introductory guide*, London: Longman.

Pedley, J.G. (1992) *Greek Art and Archaeology*, London: Cassell.

Pemberton, E.G. (1989a) *The Sanctuary of Demeter and Kore: the Greek Pottery, Corinth XVIII.1*, Princeton: American School of Classical Studies at Athens.

—— (1989b) 'The beginning of monumental painting in mainland Greece', in R.I. Curtis (ed.) *Studia Pompeiana et Classica in honor of Wilhelmina F. Jashemski*, Volume II: Classica, New York: Aristide D. Caratzas.

Perlzweig, J. (1964) *Lamps from the Athenian Agora*, Princeton: American School of Classical Studies at Athens.

Peschl, I. (1987) *Die Hetäre bei Symposion und Komos in der attisch-rotfigurigen Vasenmalerei des 6.–4. Jahrh. v. Chr.*, Frankfurt, Bern, New York: Peter Lang.

Pfuhl, E. (1923) *Malerei und Zeichnung der Griechen*, Munich: F. Bruckmann.

Phillips, K.M. (1968) 'Perseus and Andromeda', *AJA* 72: 1–23.

Pinney, G.F. (1984a) 'For the heroes are at hand', *JHS* 104: 181–3.

—— (1984b) Review of *The Berlin Painter* by D.C. Kurtz and J.D. Beazley, *AJA* 88: 419–21.

Piotrovsky, B., Galanina, L. and Grach, N. (1987) *Skythian Art*, Oxford: Phaidon and Leningrad: Aurora.

Pipili, M. (1987) *Laconian Iconography of the Sixth Century B.C.*, Oxford: Oxford University Committee for Archaeology.

Pollitt, J.J. (1972) *Art and Experience in Classical Greece*, Cambridge: Cambridge University Press.

—— (1986) *Art in the Hellenistic Age*, Cambridge: Cambridge University Press.

—— (1990) *The Art of Ancient Greece: sources and documents* (2nd edn), Cambridge: Cambridge University Press.

Prange, M. (1989) *Der Niobidenmaler und seine Werkstatt*, Frankfurt, Bern, New York, Paris: Peter Lang.

Pritchett, W.K. (1953) 'The Attic Stelai, Part I', *Hesperia* 22: 225–311

—— (1956) 'The Attic Stelai, Part II', *Hesperia* 25: 178–328.

—— (1961) 'Five new fragments of the Attic Stelai', *Hesperia* 30: 23–9.

Raab, I. (1972) *Zu den Darstellungen des Parisurteils in der griechischen Kunst*, Frankfurt and Bern: Peter and Herbert Lang.

Ramage, N.H. (1990) 'Sir William Hamilton as collector, exporter, and dealer: the acquisition and dispersal of his collections', *AJA* 94: 469–80.

—— (1992) 'Goods, graves, and scholars: 18th-century archaeologists in Britain and Italy', *AJA* 96: 653–61.

Rasmussen, T. (1985) 'Etruscan shapes in Attic pottery', *AK* 28: 33–9.

—— (1991) 'Corinth and the Orientalising phenomenon', in T. Rasmussen and N. Spivey (eds) *Looking at Greek Vases*, Cambridge: Cambridge University Press.

Rasmussen, T. and Spivey, N. (eds) (1991) *Looking at Greek Vases*, Cambridge: Cambridge University Press.

Rasponi, S. (1990) *Capolavori di Euphronios: un pioniere della ceramografia attica*, Milan: Fabbri, Bompiani, Sonzogno, Etas s.p.a.

Rathje, A. (1990) 'The adoption of the Homeric banquet in central Italy in the Orientalizing period', in O. Murray (ed.) *Sympotica: a symposium on the Symposion*, Oxford: Clarendon Press.

Reilly, J. (1989) 'Many brides: "Mistress and Maid" on Athernian lekythoi', *Hesperia* 58: 411–44.

Reynolds, L.D. and Wilson, N.G. (1991) *Scribes and Scholars: a guide to the transmission of Greek and Latin literature* (3rd edn), Oxford: Clarendon Press.

Richardson, N. (1993) *The Iliad: a commentary, Vol. VI, Books 21–24*, Cambridge: Cambridge University Press.

— Bibliography —

Richter, G.M.A. (1923) *The Craft of the Athenian Potter*, New Haven: Yale University Press.

—— (1987) *Handbook of Greek Art* (9th edn), London: Phaidon.

Richter, G.M.A. and Milne, M.J. (1935) *Shapes and Names of Athenian Vases*, New York: Metropolitan Museum of Art.

Roberts, S.R. (1978) *The Attic Pyxis*, Chicago: Ares.

Robertson, M. (1951) 'The place of vase-painting in Greek art', *ABSA* 46: 151–9.

—— (1958) 'The Gorgos cup', *AJA* 62: 55–66.

—— (1959) *Greek Painting*, Geneva: Skira.

—— (1975) *A History of Greek Art*, Cambridge: Cambridge University Press.

—— (1976) 'Beazley and after', *MJbK* 27: 29–46.

—— (1977) 'The death of Talos', *JHS* 97: 158–60.

—— (1985) 'Beazley and Attic vase painting', in D. Kurtz (ed.) *Beazley and Oxford*, Oxford: Oxford University Committee for Archaeology.

—— (1989) 'Beazley's use of terms', in T.H. Carpenter *Beazley Addenda*, Oxford: Oxford University Press.

—— (1991) 'Adopting an approach I', in T. Rasmussen and N. Spivey (eds) *Looking at Greek Vases*, Cambridge: Cambridge University Press.

—— (1992a) *The Art of Vase-Painting in Classical Athens*, Cambridge: Cambridge University Press.

—— (1992b) 'The Pioneers in context', in I. Wehgartner (ed.) *Euphronios und seine Zeit. Kolloquium in Berlin 19./20. April 1991*, Berlin: Antikensammlung Museen Preussischer Kulturbesitz.

Robinson, D.M., Mylonas, G.E., Graham, J.W. and Clement, P.A. (1929–52) *Excavations at Olynthus*, Baltimore: Johns Hopkins University Press.

Rosati, R. (ed.) (1989) *La Ceramica Attica nel Mediterraneo: Analisi Computerizzata della Diffusione, le Fasi Iniziali (630–560 B.C.)*, Bologna: Cooperativa Libraria Universitaria Editrice Bologna.

Rotroff, S.I. (1982) *Hellenistic Pottery: mouldmade bowls, Agora XXII*, Princeton: American School of Classical Studies at Athens.

—— (1991) 'Attic West Slope vase painting', *Hesperia* 60: 59–102.

Rotroff, S.I. and Oakley, J.H. (1992) 'Debris from a public dining place in the Athenian Agora', *Hesperia Supplement XXV*, Princeton: American School of Classical Studies at Athens.

Rowland, B. (1963) *The Classical Tradition in Western Art*, Cambridge, Mass.: Harvard University Press.

Ruckert, A. (1976) *Frühe Keramik Böotiens, AK Supplement X*.

Rühfel, H. (1984) *Kinderleben im klassischen Athen*, Mainz: Philipp von Zabern.

Rumpf, A. (1927) *Chalkidische Vasen*, Berlin and Leipzig: Walter de Gruyter.

Rykwert, J. (1980) *The First Moderns; the architects of the eighteenth century*, Cambridge, Mass.: MIT Press.

Saxl, F. (1940–1) 'The classical inscription in Renaissance art and politics', *JWCI* 4: 19–46.

—— (1957) *Lectures I*, London: Warburg & Courtauld Institute.

Schäfer, J. (1957), *Studien zu den griechischen Reliefpithoi des 8.–6. Jahrhunderts v. Chr. aus Kreta, Rhodos, Tenos und Boiotien*, Kallmünz: Michael Lassleben.

Schauenburg, K. (1975) 'Eurymedon Eimi', *AM* 90: 97–121.

Schefold, K. (1964) *Frühgriechische Sagenbilder*, Munich: Hirmer.

—— (1966) *Myth and Legend in Early Greek Art* (translation of the 1964 volume by Audrey Hicks), London: Thames & Hudson.

—— (1978) *Götter- und Heldensagen der Griechen in der spätarchaischen Kunst*, Munich: Hirmer.

— Bibliography —

—— (1981) *Die Göttersage in der klassichen und hellenistischen Kunst*, Munich: Hirmer.

—— (1985) 'Parisurteil der Zeit Alexanders des Grossen', *Greek Vases in the J. Paul Getty Museum 2 (OPA 3)*: 119–26.

—— (1988) (with F. Jung) *Die Urkönige, Perseus, Bellerophon, Herakles und Theseus in der klassischen und hellenistischen Kunst*, Munich: Hirmer.

—— (1989) (with F. Jung) *Die Sagen von den Argonauten, von Theben und Troia in der klassischen und hellenistischen Kunst*, Munich: Hirmer.

—— (1992) *Gods and Heroes in Late Archaic Greek Art* (translation of the 1978 volume by Alan Griffiths), Cambridge: Cambridge University Press.

—— (1993) *Götter- und Heldensagen der Griechen in der Früh- und Hocharchaischen Kunst*, Munich: Hirmer.

Scheibler, I. (1983) *Griechische Töpferkunst*, Munich: Beck.

—— (1994) *Griechische Malerei der Antike*, Munich: Beck.

Schiering, W. (1957) *Werkstätten orientalisierender Keramik auf Rhodos*, Berlin: Gebr. Mann.

Schmidt, M., Trendall, A.D. and Cambitoglou, A. (1976) *Eine Gruppe apulischer Grabvasen in Basel: Studien zu Gehalt und Form der unteritalischen Sepulkralkunst*, Mainz: Philipp von Zabern.

Schmitt Pantel, P. (1992) *La cité au banquet: histoire des repas publics dans les cités grecques*, Rome: École française.

Schweitzer, B. (1971) *Greek Geometric Art*, London: Phaidon.

Seeberg, A. (1971) *Corinthian Komos Vases (BICS Supplement 19)*, London: Institute of Classical Studies, University of London.

—— (1994) '*Epoiesen, egrapsen*, and the organization of the vase trade', *JHS* 114: 162–4.

Sforzini, C. (1989) 'Deux français à Vulci au XIXe Siècle: Lucien Bonaparte, Prince de Canino et Stéphane Gsell', in M. Cébeillac-Gervasoni, P. Chambon and D. Hugon (eds) *Les Étrusques à Vulci: le peintre de Micali et son monde*, Clermont-Ferrand: Maison Départementale de l'Innovation.

Shapiro, H.A. (1989a) 'Two black-figure neck-amphorae in the J. Paul Getty Museum: problems of workshop and iconography', *Greek Vases in the J. Paul Getty Museum 4 (OPA 5)*: 11–32.

—— (1989b) *Art and Cult Under the Tyrants of Athens*, Mainz: Philipp von Zabern.

—— (1991) 'Theseus: aspects of the hero in archaic Greece', in D. Buitron-Oliver (ed.) *New Perspectives in Early Greek Art*, Washington: National Gallery of Art.

—— (1993) *Personifications in Greek Art: the representation of abstract concepts, 600–400 B.C.*, Kilchberg/Zürich: Akanthus.

—— (1994) *Myth into Art: poet and painter in classical Greece*, London and New York: Routledge.

Shapley, R.F. (1920) 'A student of ancient ceramics, Antonio Pollajolo', *Art Bulletin* 2: 78–86.

Shefton, B.B. (1954) 'Three Laconian vase painters', *ABSA* 49: 299–310.

—— (1989) 'The Auge bowl', in B.F. Cook (ed.) *The Rogozen Treasure. Papers of the Anglo-Bulgarian Conference, 12 March 1987*, London: British Museum Publications.

Simon, E. (1967) 'Boreas und Oreithyia auf dem silbernen Rhyton in Triest', *Antike und Abenland* 13: 101–27.

—— (1982) 'Satyr-plays on vases in the time of Aeschylus', in D. Kurtz and B. Sparkes (eds) *The Eye of Greece*, Cambridge: Cambridge University Press.

—— (1983) *The Festivals of Attica: an archaeological commentary*, Madison: University of Wisconsin Press.

Simon, E. and Hirmer, M. (1976/1981) *Die Griechische Vasen*, Munich: Hirmer.

Sklenář, K. (1983) *Archaeology in Central Europe: the first 500 years*, Leicester: Leicester University Press.

Small, J.P. (1991/2) 'The Etruscan view of Greek art', *Boreas* 14/15: 51–65.

—— (1994) 'Scholars, Etruscans, and Attic painted vases', *JRA* 7: 34–58.

Snodgrass, A.M. (1971) *The Dark Age of Greece*, Edinburgh: Edinburgh University Press.

—— (1979) 'Poet and painter in eighth century Greece', *PCPS* 205: 118–30.

—— (1980) 'Towards an interpretation of the Geometric figure-scenes', *AM* 95: 51–8.

—— (1987) *An Archaeology of Greece*, Berkeley and Los Angeles: University of California Press.

Sourvinou-Inwood, C. (1971) 'Theseus lifting the rock and a cup near the Pithos Painter', *JHS* 91: 94–109.

—— (1990) 'Myths as images: Theseus and Medea as a case study', in L. Edwards (ed.) *Approaches to Greek Myth*, Baltimore: Johns Hopkins University Press.

—— (1991) *'Reading' Greek culture: text and images, rituals and myths*, Oxford: Clarendon Press.

—— (1995) *'Reading' Greek death: to the end of the classical period*, Oxford: Clarendon Press.

Sparkes, B.A. (1962) 'The Greek kitchen', *JHS* 82: 121–37.

—— (1965) 'The Greek kitchen: addenda', *JHS* 85: 162–3.

—— (1975) 'Illustrating Aristophanes', *JHS* 95: 122–35.

—— (1976) 'Treading the grapes', *BABesch* 51: 47–64.

—— (1981) 'Not cooking, but baking', *Greece and Rome* 28: 172–8.

—— (1985) 'Aspects of Onesimos', in C.G. Boulter (ed.) *Greek Art: Archaic into Classical, a symposion held at the University of Cincinnati April 2–3 1982*, Leiden: Brill.

—— (1991a) *Greek Pottery: an introduction*, Manchester: Manchester University Press.

—— (1991b) *Greek Art* (Greece and Rome New Surveys in the Classics no. 22), Oxford: Oxford University Press.

—— (1994) 'Classical art', in J. Boardman (ed.) *The Cambridge Ancient History, Plates to Volumes V and VI The Fifth and Fourth Centuries B.C.*, Cambridge: Cambridge University Press

Sparkes, B.A. and Talcott, L. (1970) *Black and Plain Pottery of the Sixth, Fifth and Fourth Centuries B.C.: The Athenian Agora XII*, Princeton: American School of Classical Studies at Athens.

Spivey, N. (1991) 'Greek vases in Etruria', in T. Rasmussen and N. Spivey (eds) *Looking at Greek Vases*, Cambridge: Cambridge University Press.

Spivey, N. and Stoddard, S. (1990) *Etruscan Italy*, London: B.T. Batsford.

Stewart, A. (1983) 'Stesichoros and the François vase', in W.G. Moon (ed.) *Ancient Greek Art and Iconography*, Madison: University of Wisconsin Press.

Stibbe, C.M. (1972) *Lakonische Vasenmalerei des sechsten Jahrhunderts v. Chr.*, Amsterdam and London: North-Holland Publishing Company.

—— (1991) 'Bellerophon and the Chimaira on a Lakonian Cup by the Boreads Painter', *Greek Vases in the Getty Nuseum* 5 (OPA 7): 5–12.

Stinton, T.C.W. (1965/1990) *Euripides and the Judgement of Paris*, London: Society for the Promotion of Hellenic Studies, and (1990) in *Collected Papers on Greek Tragedy*, Oxford: Clarendon Press.

Tanner, J. (1994) 'Shifting paradigms in Classical art history', *Antiquity* 68: 650–5.

Taplin, O. (1993) *Comic Angels and Other Approaches to Greek Drama through Vase-Paintings*, Oxford: Clarendon Press.

Taylor, T., Vickers, M., Morphy, H. (1994) 'Is there a place for aesthetics in archaeology?', *CAJ* 4: 249–69.

Themelis, P.G. (1971) *Brauron: guide to the site and museum*, Athens: Apollo Editions.

Thompson, D.B. (1949) 'Ostrakina Toreumata', *Hesperia Supplement VIII*: 365–72.

—— (1971) *The Athenian Agora: an ancient shopping center*, Princeton: American School of Classical Studies at Athens.

Thompson, H.A. (1934/1987) 'Two centuries of Hellenistic pottery', *Hesperia* 3: 311–480. Reissued in 1987 in H.A. Thompson and D.B. Thompson, *Hellenistic Pottery and Terracottas*, with redating and updated bibliography by S. Rotroff, Princeton: American School of Classical Studies at Athens.

—— (1984) 'The Athenian vase-painters and their neighbors', in P.M. Rice (ed.) *Pots and Potters: current approaches in ceramic archaeology*, Los Angeles: University of California Press.

Thompson, H.A. and Wycherley, R.E. (1972) *The Agora of Athens: The Athenian Agora XIV*, Princeton: American School of Classical Studies at Athens.

Tillyard, E.M.W. (1923) *The Hope Vases*, Cambridge: Cambridge University Press.

Tischbein, W. (1791–5) *Collection of Engravings from Ancient Vases mostly of Pure Greek Workmanship, discovered in Sepulchres in the Kingdom of the Two Sicilies*, Naples: W. Tischbein.

Touchefeu-Meynier, O. (1968) *Thèmes Odysséens dans l'art antique*, Paris: de Boccard.

Trendall, A.D. (1967) *The Red-Figured Vases of Lucania, Campania and Sicily*, Oxford: Clarendon Press.

—— (1971) *Gli indigeni nella pittura italiota*, Taranto, exhibition catalogue.

—— (1983) *Third (Consolidated) Supplement to The Red-Figured Vases of Lucania, Campania and Sicily (BICS Supplement 41)*, London: Institute of Classical Studies, University of London.

—— (1987) *The Red-Figured Vases of Paestum*, Rome: British School in Rome.

—— (1989) *Red Figure Vases of South Italy and Sicily*, London: Thames & Hudson.

—— (1991) 'Farce and tragedy in South Italian vase-painting', in T. Rasmussen and N. Spivey (eds) *Looking at Greek Vases*, Cambridge: Cambridge University Press.

Trendall, A.D. and Cambitoglou, A. (1978) *The Red-Figured Vases of Apulia I*, Oxford: Clarendon Press.

—— (1982) *The Red-Figured Vases of Apulia II*, Oxford: Clarendon Press.

—— (1983) *First Supplement to The Red-Figured Vases of Apulia (BICS Supplement 42)*, London: Institute of Classical Studies, University of London.

—— (1991–2) *Second Supplement to The Red-Figured Vases of Apulia (BICS Supplement 60)*, London: Institute of Classical Studies, University of London.

Trendall, A.D. and Webster, T.B.L. (1971) *Illustrations of Greek Drama*, London: Phaidon.

Trias de Arribas, G. (1967–8) *Ceramicas Griegas de la Peninsula Iberica*, Valencia: Domenech S.A.

True, M. (ed.) (1987) *Papers on the Amasis Painter and His World*, Malibu: J. Paul Getty Museum.

Turner, N. (ed.) (1993) *The Paper Museum of Cassiano dal Pozzo*, Milan: Olivetti.

Tyrrell, W.B. (1984) *Amazons: a study of Athenian mythmaking*, Baltimore and London: Johns Hopkins University Press.

Ure, A.D. (1936) 'Red figure cups with incised and stamped decoration I', *JHS* 56: 204–15.

—— (1944) 'Red figure cups with incised and stamped decoration II', *JHS* 64: 67–77.

Vaizey, M. (1988) 'More to see than meets the eye', *Sunday Times* 16 October: C 10.

Vanderpool, E. (1980) 'The state prison of ancient Athens', in K. de Vries (ed.) *From Athens to Gordion. The Papers of a Memorial Symposium for Rodney S. Young*, Philadelphia: University Museum, University of Pennsylvania.

van Hoorn, G. (1951) *Choes and Anthesteria*, Leiden: Brill.

Vasari, G. (1991) *Le vite dei più eccellenti pittori, scultori e architetti*, Rome: Grandi Tascabili Economici Newton.

Vermeule, C.C. (1958) 'Aspects of scientific archaeology in the seventeenth century', *Proceedings of American Philosophical Society* 102: 193–214.

—— (1964) *European Art and the Classical Past*, Cambridge, Mass.: Harvard University Press.

Vermeule, E.T. (1965) 'Fragments of a symposion by Euphronios', *AK* 8: 34–9.

—— (1991) 'Myth and tradition from Mycenae to Homer', in D. Buitron-Oliver (ed.) *New Perspectives in Early Greek Art*, Washington: National Gallery of Art.

Vermeule, E.T. and Karageorghis, V. (1982) *Mycenaean Pictorial Vase Painting*, Cambridge, Mass. and London: Harvard University Press.

Vickers, M. (1977) 'A Greek source for Pollaiuolo's Battle of the Nudes and Hercules and the Twelve Giants', *Art Bulletin* 59: 182–7.

—— (1978) *Greek Symposia*, London: Joint Association of Classical Teachers.

—— (1985) 'Artful crafts: the influence of metalwork on Athenian painted pottery', *JHS* 105: 108–28.

—— (1985–6) 'Imaginary Etruscans: changing perceptions of Etruria since the fifteenth century', *Hephaistos* 7–8: 153–68.

—— (1987) 'Value and simplicity: eighteenth-century taste and the study of Greek vases', *Past & Present* 116: 98–137.

Vickers, M. and Gill, D. (1994) *Artful Crafts: ancient Greek silverware and pottery*, Oxford: Clarendon Press.

Vickers, M., Impey, O. and Allan, J. (1986) *From Silver to Ceramic: the painter's debt to metalwork in the Graeco-Roman, Oriental and Islamic worlds*, Oxford: Ashmolean Museum.

Vierneisel, K. and Kaeser, B. (1990) *Kunst der Schale, Kultur des Trinkens*, Munich: Staatliche Antikensammlungen und Glyptothek.

Vitelli, K. (1992) 'Pots vs. vases', *Antiquity* 66: 550–3.

Vojatzi, M. (1982) *Frühe Argonautenbilder*, Würzburg: Konrad Triltsch.

von Bothmer, D. (1972) 'A unique pair of Attic vases', *RA*: 83–92.

—— (1976) 'Der Euphronioskrater in New York', *AA*: 485–512.

—— (1977) 'Les vases de la collection Campana: un exemple de collaboration avec le Metropolitan Museum', *Revue du Louvre* 27: 213–21.

—— (1981a) 'The Death of Sarpedon', in S.L. Hyatt (ed.) *The Greek Vase*, Latham, New York: Hudson-Mohawk Association of Colleges and Universities.

—— (1981b) '῎Αμασις ᾽Αμάσιδος', *GettyMusJ* 9: 1–4.

—— (1981c) 'A new Kleitias fragment from Egypt', *AK* 24: 66–7.

—— (1985a) *The Amasis Painter and His World: vase-painting in sixth century B.C. Athens*, Malibu: J. Paul Getty Museum, and London: Thames & Hudson.

—— (1985b) 'Beazley the teacher', in D. Kurtz (ed.) *Beazley and Oxford*, Oxford: Oxford University Committee for Archaeology.

—— (1987) 'Greek vase-painting: two hundred years of connoisseurship', in M. True (ed.) *Papers on the Amasis Painter and His World*, Malibu: J. Paul Getty Museum.

von Bothmer, D. and Milne, M.J. (1947) 'The Taleides amphora', *MMA Bulletin* 5: 221–8.

Walker, H.J. (1995) *Theseus and Athens*, New York: Oxford University Press.

Wasbinski, Z. (1968) 'Portrait d'un amateur d'art de la Renaissance', *Arte Veneta* 22: 21–9.

Webster, T.B.L. (1972) *Potter and Patron in Classical Athens*, London: Metheun.

Wehgartner, I. (1983) *Attisch Weissgrundige Keramik*, Mainz: Philipp von Zabern.

—— (ed.) (1992) *Euphronios und seine Zeit. Kolloquium in Berlin 19./20. April 1991*, Berlin: Staatliche Museen Preussicher Kulturbesitz.

Weill, N. and Salviat, F. (1960) 'Un plat du VIIe siècle à Thasos: Bellérophon et la Chimère', *BCH* 84: 347–86.

Weiss, R. (1969) *The Renaissance Discovery of Classical Antiquity*, Oxford: Blackwell.

Whitbread, I.K. (1995) *Greek Transport Amphorae: a petrological and archaeological study* (Fitch Laboratory Occasional Paper 4), Athens: British School at Athens.

Whitley, J. (1994) 'Protoattic pottery: a contextual approach', in I. Morris (ed.) *Classical Greece: ancient histories and modern archaeologies*, Cambridge: Cambridge University Press.

Williams, D. (1983a) 'Sophilos in the British Museum', *Greek Vases in the J. Paul Getty Museum 1 (OPA 1)*: 9–34.

—— (1983b/1993) 'Women on Athenian vases: problems of interpretation', in A. Cameron and A. Kuhrt (eds) *Images of Women in Antiquity*, London: Croom Helm/Routledge.

—— (1985) *Greek Vases*, London: British Museum Publications.

—— (1991a) 'The invention of the red figure technique and the race between vase-painting and free painting', in T. Rasmussen and N. Spivey (eds) *Looking at Greek Vases*, Cambridge: Cambridge University Press.

—— (1991b) 'Onesimos and the Getty Iliupersis' *Greek Vases in the J. Paul Getty Museum 5 (OPA 7)*: 41–64.

—— (1992) 'The Brygos Tomb reassembled and 19th-century commerce in Capuan antiquities', *AJA* 96: 617–36.

—— (1995) 'Potter, painter and purchaser', in A. Verbanck-Piérard and D. Viviers (eds) *Culture et Cité: l'avènement d'Athènes à l'époque archaïque*, Brussels: Fondation Archéologique de l'U.L.B.

—— (forthcoming) 'Refiguring Attic red-figure'.

Wind, E. (1963) *Art and Anarchy*, London: Faber & Faber.

Wintermeyer, U. (1975) 'Die polychrome Reliefkeramik aus Centuripe', *JDAI* 90: 136–241.

Wollheim (1974) *On Art and the Mind*, London and Cambridge, Mass.: Harvard University Press.

Wood, C. (1983) *Olympian Dreamers: Victorian Classical painters 1860–1914*, London: Constable.

Woodford, S. (1993) *The Trojan War in Ancient Art*, London: Duckworth.

Yuen, T. (1979) 'Giulio Romano, Giovanni da Udine and Raphael: some influences from the minor arts of antiquity' *JWCI* 42: 263–72.

Zamarchi Grassi, P. (1992) 'Osservazioni sul restauro del cratere di Arezzo con qualche nota di carattere antiquario', in M. Cygielman, M. Iozzo, F. Nicosia and P. Zamarchi Grassi (eds) *Euphronios: Atti del Seminario Internazionale di Studi, Arezzo 27–28 Maggio 1990*, Florence and Milan: Il Ponte.

Ziomecki, J. (1975) *Les représentations d'artisans sur les vases antiques*, Warsaw: Polish Academy of Sciences.

SUBJECT INDEX

MUSEUM INDEX OF VASES
ILLUSTRATED

—— •◆• ——

Ampurias, Museum
Corinthian black-figure: Fig. VI: 22
Athens, the Agora Excavations
Athenian black and patterned:
MC 250 Fig. III: 8; MC 373 Fig.
III; 8; MC 781 Fig. III: 8; MC 937
Fig. III: 8; MC 938 Fig. III: 8;
MC 948 Fig. III: 8; P 2285 Fig. I:
22; P 5117 Fig. III: 14; P 10548
Fig. VI: 1; P 12551 Fig. III: 6
Athenian red-figure: P 24113 Fig.
IV: 8
Athenian West Slope: P 599 Fig. I:
20
coarse: MC 328-331 Fig. III: 8;
P 1207 Fig. III: 2; P 19120 Fig. III:
16; P 19845 Fig. III: 10; P 20558
Fig. III: 2; P 20813 Fig. III: 10;
P 21947 Fig. III: 10; P 23188 Fig.
III: 10; P 24864 Fig. III: 10;
P 24913 Fig. III: 10; SS 7319 Fig.
III: 16; SS 7918 Fig. III: 16;
SS 8602 Fig. III: 16
mould made: P 28544 Fig. I: 21
plain: P 2084 Fig. III: 14; P 3559 Fig.
III: 14; P 8586 Fig. III: 6; P 9445
Fig. III: 8; P 13429 Fig. III: 14;
P 16774 Fig. III: 11; P 16720 Fig.
III: 6; P 18605 Fig. III: 8; P 25757
Fig. III: 11
stone: ST 193 Fig. III: 6; ST 201 Fig.
III: 6

Athens, Kerameikos Museum
plain: inv. 5040 (WP 13, Grave 55)
Fig. VI: 4
contents of offering ditch: Fig. III:
3

Athens, Epigraphical Museum
inscription: 6763 Fig. VI: 2

Athens, National Museum
Athenian black-figure: 15155, Acr.
611a Fig. VI: 13
Athenian red-figure: Acr. 609 Fig. IV:
1; 1629 Fig. III: 4
Athenian white-ground: 1818 Fig. I:
12

Basel, Antikenmuseum
Apulian red-figure: S 21 Fig. V: 12
Athenian red-figure: BS 440 Fig. IV:
10
Sicilian red-figure: BS 478 Fig. I: 14

Berlin, Antikensammlung, Preussischer
Kulturbesitz
Athenian red-figure: F 2291 Fig. V: 8;
F 2298 Fig. III: 17; inv. 3223 Fig.
V: 11
Campanian black: inv. 30017 Fig. I:
23
Corinthian black-figure: inv. 4856
Fig. II: 4
Paestan red-figure: F 3044 Fig. V: 3

Berne, Historical Museum
Athenian red-figure: 12227 Fig. III:
5

Boston, Museum of Fine Arts
Athenian red-figure: 00.354 Fig. VI:
9; 10.179 Fig. IV: 9

Brauron, Museum
Attic white-figure: A 25 Fig. VI: 14

Palermo, Museo Nazionale
Athenian black-figure and red-figure:
V 650 Fig. I: 10

Paris, Louvre
Athenian red-figure: G 152 Fig. II:
6
Corinthian black-figure: E 635 Fig.
VI: 18
Rhodian: CA 350 (E 658) Fig. I: 4

Plovdiv, Archaeological Museum
silver-gilt: 1516 Fig. VI: 8

Richmond (Virginia), Museum of Fine
Arts
Apulian red-figure: 80.162 Fig. I: 15

Rome, Vatican Museum
Athenian red-figure: 16571 Fig. IV:
5

Rome, Villa Giulia Museum
Protocorinthian: 22679 Fig. V: 7

Sofia, Archaeological Museum
silver and silver-gilt: inv. 22301-22465
Fig. VI: 5; inv. 22304 Fig. VI: 11

Thessaloniki, Museum
bronze: Fig. VI: 6

Toledo, Museum of Art
Lucanian red-figure: 1981.110 Fig. I:
16